Understanding Muslim-West Alienation:

Building a Better Future

Understanding Muslim-West Alienation:

Building a Better Future

Arshad Khan

Writers Club Press

San Jose New York Lincoln Shanghai

Understanding Muslim-West Alienation:
Building a Better Future

All Rights Reserved © 2002 by Arshad Khan

No part of this book may be reproduced or transmitted in any form or by any means, graphic, electronic, or mechanical, including photocopying, recording, taping, or by any information storage retrieval system, without the permission in writing from the publisher.

Writers Club Press
an imprint of iUniverse, Inc.

For information address:
iUniverse, Inc.
5220 S. 16th St., Suite 200
Lincoln, NE 68512
www.iuniverse.com

ISBN: 0-595-23709-6

Printed in the United States of America

Contents

PREFACE xi
INTRODUCTION xiii
TERMINOLOGY xv

CHAPTER 1: EVOLUTION AND RISE OF ISLAM 1
EVOLUTION OF ISLAM 1
Historical roots 1
Periodic reinforcement and revival 2
Religion is formalized 2
RISE AND SPREAD OF ISLAM 2
Where and how the religion spread 2
622-632: Period under Muhammad 3
632-661: Period under the four caliphs 3
661-750: Period under the Ummayyad dynasty 4
750-1258: Period under the Abbassid dynasty 5
750-950: Golden Age of Islam 6
ISLAM'S CONTRIBUTION AND IMPACT 7
Dignity 7
Islamic civilization 7
Global influence 8
Nurturer of knowledge during the Dark Ages 8
Areas of excellence and contribution 9

CHAPTER 2: DECLINE OF ISLAMIC CIVILIZATION AND PRESENT STATUS 11
DECLINE OF MUSLIM DYNASTIES AND EMPIRES 11
    How the decline occurred 11
    End of the Abbassid dynasty 11
    Fatimid dynasty 12
    Seljuk Turks 12
    Mongols 13
    Fall of Spain in 1492 13
    End of the Safavid Empire 14
    End of the Mughal Empire 14
    End of the Ottoman Empire 14
MODERN WORLD EVENTS AND DEVELOPMENTS 15
    Colonial subjugation 15
    Major 20th-century developments 16
        Balfour Declaration sows seeds of future conflict 16
        Islamic states are formed 17
ISLAM IN TODAY'S WORLD 18
    Widespread underdeveloped Muslim societies 18
    Population 18
    Areas of concentration 19
    Ethnic diversity 20
    Cultural diversity 20
    Political diversity 20
    Myth of unity and brotherhood 20
    Common misconception about Arabs and Muslims 21
ISLAM IN AMERICA 21
    History of Islam in America 21
    Population 22
    Dynamic community 23

CHAPTER 3: DEFINING EVENTS AND HOW MUSLIMS VIEW THEM ...25
HISTORICAL EVENTS ...25
Introduction ...25
Decline of Islamic civilization after its Golden Age ...26
Crusades ...26
Failed Turkish siege of Vienna ...26
End of the Ottoman Empire ...27
Revival and reform movements ...27
End of the colonial era ...28
Saudi Arabia comes under the Saud family rule ...29
EVENTS AFTER 1947 ...29
Partition of India ...29
Kashmir ...30
Palestine ...32
Overthrow of Mossadegh in Iran ...32
Arab defeats in four wars ...33
1973 oil embargo ...34
Soviet Union's defeat in Afghanistan ...34
Breakup of the Soviet Union ...35
Gulf War ...35
Bosnia massacres ...36
Beirut, Somalia, and South Lebanon ...36
Financial crises ...37
    Saudi Arabia ...37
    Bank of Credit and Commerce ...38
Leadership losses ...39
Pakistan's nuclear bomb ...40

CHAPTER 4: PERCEIVED WESTERN ROLE AND MUSLIM REACTION ...41
ROLE PLAYED BY AMERICA AND WESTERN POWERS ...41

Support for Israel 41
Soft attitude towards Israeli leadership 43
Support for despots and dictators 44
Judging by, and imposing, foreign values 44
Insensitivity to Muslim feelings 45
Hatred for the American way of life 45
Media bias 45
Friendship of convenience 46
Double standards 47
Post-Gulf War Iraq policy 48
Not differentiating between terrorism and freedom struggles 49
Divide and rule 50
Islamic bomb 51

REACTION BY MUSLIMS TO RECENT
HISTORICAL EVENTS 52
Refusing to accept responsibility 52
Advocating return to the seventh century 52
Feeling victimized 53
Passive hatred 53
Acting prejudiced 54
Becoming freedom fighters or terrorists 54
Exporting mujahideen and terrorists 55

9-11: THE HIJACKING OF ISLAM 56
Why it happened 56
Anti-Islamic act 57
How Muslims view the 9-11 tragedy 57
Impact on Muslims 58

CHAPTER 5: WHERE LIES THE TRUTH 59
ANALYZING MUSLIM COMPLAINTS AGAINST AMERICA 60
American support for Israel is one-sided 60
Jewish influence in the Senate is too strong 61

Palestine issue incorrectly projected as religious struggle 62
America is anti-Islam and anti-Muslim 63
Support for despots and dictators 64
Judging by, and imposing, foreign values 65
Insensitivity to Muslim feelings 66
Hatred for the American way of life 67
American media is biased 68
News is driven by business needs 70
Mujahideen were used and abandoned 71
Friendship of convenience 72
Policy implemented by inexperienced politicians 73
Uninformed Americans 74
Slow response to Bosnian crisis 75
Guilty by association 76
British influence and bias 77
ANALYZING MUSLIM ISSUES AND FAILURES 78
Lack of education is widespread 78
Priorities are wrong 79
Religious extremists in control 80
Religion used as a cover to achieve ends 81
Palestine incorrectly portrayed as a religious struggle 82
Kuwait crisis was initiated by Iraq, not America 83
Bhutto was responsible for his own downfall 84
Saudi non-oil exports have started creating major problems 84
Poor communications and use of media 85
Muslims lack role models 86
Majority is silent 87
Leadership has failed consistently 87
Jehad hijacked 88

CHAPTER 6: FAILURE OF MUSLIM LEADERSHIP 89
POLITICAL LEADERSHIP 89

Organization of Islamic Conference 89
Arabs 90
Iran 91
Pakistan 92
Indonesia 93
Revolutionary: Algeria and Afghanistan 93
RELIGIOUS LEADERSHIP 94
Saudi Arabia 94
Iran 95
World 96
America 96

CHAPTER 7: JEHAD HIJACKED 99
VIOLENCE, COMPULSION, AND WAR 99
Does Islam preach violence 99
Is Islam tolerant 101
Perception of Islamic intolerance: a disconnect 102
Why Muslim tolerance has declined 104
When Islam permits war 104
JEHAD 105
Concept and purpose of jehad 105
Misconception about jehad 106
When war or armed action can be justified as jehad 107
Unholy wars 107
TERRORISM 108
Islamic view of terrorism 108
Both state-sponsored and individual acts of
terrorism are un-Islamic 109
Suicide bombing and martyrdom 110
Is Islam responsible for terrorism carried out in its name 111
FUNDAMENTALISM 112
What is fundamentalism 112

What Islamic fundamentalism represents 112
Who and where are the Muslim fundamentalists 113
What has swelled the ranks of fundamentalists 113

CHAPTER 8: BUILDING A BETTER FUTURE 115
WHAT WORLD MUSLIMS NEED TO DO 115
Address root causes of problems 115
Prioritize correctly 115
Recognize Israel 116
Stress educational, scientific, and technological development 116
Achieve economic independence 117
Introduce social reform 117
Strive for unity 118
Shift from negative to positive objectives 118
Become more responsible 119
Learn to help themselves 119
Become politically active 119
Pick good leaders and make them accountable 120
Silent majority should become vocal 120
Avoid self-righteous superiority syndrome 121
Communicate with non-Muslims 121
WHAT AMERICA AND THE WEST NEED TO DO 121
Address root causes of problems 121
Be a fair peace broker and guarantee Israel's security 122
Be informed and sensitive 122
Plan for the long-term 123
Match actions to words 124
Be unbiased and fair 124
Do not paint all with the same brush 125
Engage Muslims 125
Build on common values 125

WHAT AMERICAN MUSLIMS NEED TO DO 126
Assume world leadership 126
Leave baggage behind 126
Focus on the bigger picture 127
Put own house in order 127
Avoid double standards 128
Lead by example and marginalize extremists 128
Plan for the long-term 129
Be involved in the political process 129
Master communication techniques 130
Stress common values 130
Develop mirror image of society professionals 130
Appreciate what America has provided 131
Reach out for a better future 131

APPENDIX: CHRONOLOGY OF HISTORICAL EVENTS 133
INDEX 137
ABOUT THE AUTHOR 163

PREFACE

September 11, 2001, changed America. It brought home to Americans something they had heard about but never really experienced. The resulting American attack on al-Qaeda in Afghanistan has been delivering justice to the 9-11 perpetrators and, hopefully, the terrorists will not be able to operate as before. However, we Americans have lost on an important front. Our cherished freedom has become a victim—a victory for the terrorists. Unless real security returns, not due to the security apparatus but through genuine peace and justice, we cannot hope to return to a semblance of the good old days. New security requirements are necessary in the short-term, but they cannot provide the lasting solution. What needs to be done is to remove the root causes of the issues that cause Muslims to perceive America so negatively. The solutions lie with various governments, religious organizations and, most importantly, individual Muslims and Americans.

Understanding Muslim-West Alienation: Building a Better Future analyzes the present conflict between Muslims and the West, particularly America. It identifies and analyzes events, starting from the time Islam was introduced 14 centuries ago, that have shaped Muslim thinking and attitudes towards the West and America. It also examines the rise and fall of the Islamic civilization, empires, and dynasties as well as the factors that have led to the present depressed condition of Muslims worldwide.

In addition to historical and current events, specific Muslim complaints against the West and America, as well as the root causes of the problems between them, are identified and discussed. Both sides in this conflict have failures and mistakes, both historical and current, and both sides maintain many incorrect perceptions and biases. With the objective of building bridges for a better and more peaceful future, this book recommends actions that both sides can take.

Due to the large number of topics covered in this book, it is not possible to discuss each event, crisis, and topic in depth. I encourage your reading other works to enlarge your knowledge of any topic touched on here.

INTRODUCTION

The objective of *Understanding Muslim-West Alienation: Building a Better Future* is to inform ordinary Americans about the various issues that have caused Muslim-West alienation in a summarized, easy-to-read format. It is not an academic work to be used as a research tool by academicians and scholars. The intent is to identify historical as well as current events and issues, positive and negative, which have led to the current antagonistic situation between America and many Muslims. The ultimate aim is to build bridges between Muslims and America. With that in mind, I end this discussion with recommendations regarding what Muslims and the West can do to end this unfortunate conflict.

I realize that, with some exceptions, individual events have not created the current perception of the West and America among Muslims. It is the cumulative effect of many events that have shaped Muslim thinking and beliefs. Although some may disagree with the interpretation and analysis of individual events presented here, the overall picture remains unchanged. Rather than fixing attention on any particular event, I hope you will view the current situation, in the context of historical events, from the "ten-thousand-foot level."

Please keep the following in mind as you read this book:

- Each section is deliberately concise. I realize that most ordinary people do not have time for extensive reading. Therefore, I encourage you to refer to the numerous comprehensive books available to gain in-depth knowledge regarding a particular event or issue.

- I recognize that there can be disagreement regarding some items. For example, this book states the number of people murdered by Hafez al-Assad's military in Hama as ten thousand. However, the reported number of victims ranges from ten thousand to thirty-eight thousand. Similarly, the reported number of Kashmiri civilians killed by the Indian forces ranges from thirty-three thousand to eighty thousand while the number of Palestinian civilians reported killed at the Sabra and Shatila camps ranges from eight hundred to two thousand. Such variations can never be reconciled because there is no way for the numbers to be authenticated. What is important is to realize that the killings took place and that the magnitude of the massacres or killings does not decrease the severity of the crime nor its impact on the survivors.

I fully expect to be taken to task by the prejudiced and extremists on both sides. However, in order to be impartial it was essential that the mistakes, injustices, and false perceptions of both sides be pointed out. Unless such mistakes are acknowledged, there can be no progress toward better understanding between America and Muslims. The time has come when the past, and finger pointing, should be abandoned and a new beginning attempted.

TERMINOLOGY

- caliph: Leader of an Islamic polity, regarded as Prophet Muhammad's successor.
- Islam: Religion started by Adam, the first man, and formalized by Muhammad^p, the last prophet. The superscript "p" is a short form for "peace and blessings be upon him" which Muslims recite each time the name of Prophet Muhammad is invoked.
- jehad: The most common form is a person's inner personal struggle to be righteous. In extreme cases, it can involve the laying down of one's life for the right cause, such as the defense of Islam.
- Kaaba: Cube-shaped structure in Mecca towards which Muslims face when performing their ritual prayers. Built as place of worship by Prophet Adam and rebuilt by Prophet Abraham.
- madrassa: Islamic religious seminary.
- Muhammad: Prophet who formalized the religion of Islam.
- mujahideen: Muslim fighters who take up arms in defense of Islam, Muslims or a righteous cause.
- mullah: Local religious leader.
- Muslim: Person who follows the religion of Islam (one who submits to the will of God).
- Palestinians: Arabs who live in Palestine.
- Sharia: Islamic law.
- Shia: Minority sect of Islam primarily concentrated in Iran and Iraq.
- sultan: Ruler of a Muslim country, especially of the former Turkish Ottoman Empire.

CHAPTER 1

EVOLUTION AND RISE OF ISLAM

EVOLUTION OF ISLAM

Historical roots

According to Islam, Adam and Eve were the first human beings created by God. When He sent them to live on Earth, He instructed them to obey His commandments, follow His guidance, and worship Him. They were told to "submit to the will of God," which is what the word *Islam* means. In accordance with His instructions, Adam and Eve led a life on Earth in conformity with God's will. Their submission to God marks the beginning of Islam, according to its adherents. Nowadays, when reference is made to Islam, it means the religion taught by Prophet Muhammad of Arabia.

Periodic reinforcement and revival

After Adam, God periodically sent prophets to various nations and countries. They were instrumental in leading their people to the "right" path—monotheism and obedience to God. However, after the death of a prophet, it was typical for nations to drift back to an old way of life based on polytheism and other activities that conflicted with God's commands. To reinforce the message and revive the religion, God periodically sent prophets for thousands of years.

Every prophet sent after Adam delivered the same message and guidance. According to Muslims, all prophets including Noah, Abraham, David, Moses, and Jesus submitted to the will of God and, hence, followed Islam. Although prophets brought specific messages tailored to the unique issues and times of their own people, they never deviated from the primary message of Islam—submission to God.

Religion is formalized

In the year 610, Muhammad became a prophet in Arabia at the age of 40. Initially, he encountered stiff resistance and persecution. By the time he died in 632, he had formalized the religion of Islam and established an Islamic society and state. According to Islam, Muhammad is the last prophet and no more prophets will follow him. Therefore, the form of Islam that he preached and formalized, as per Islamic teachings, will remain unchanged till the end of time.

RISE AND SPREAD OF ISLAM

Where and how the religion spread

Islam spread rapidly after it was introduced in Arabia. In less than a century, an Islamic Empire had spread across the Middle East and North Africa. Its reach extended from Spain in the west to Central Asia and China in the east. Muslim forces reached France, within 170 miles of Paris, but were defeated in 732 at the Battle of Tours. In 1529, Islamic forces laid siege to Vienna but failed to capture it.

During the early days of Islam, the driving force for expansion was the desire to spread the religion. Force was used when resistance was encountered, though the vanquished were not compelled to accept Islam. When Umar, the Islamic head of state, entered Jerusalem in 638, he made the Covenant of Umar, which guaranteed Christians freedom of religion, use of their places of worship, and the right to visit their holy places. For the Jews, he promised religious freedom and cancelled the Roman decree that had barred them from entering Jerusalem.

The initial expansion of the Islamic Empire was due to its military strength. However, its expansion also required the conquering forces to become involved in the day-to-day administration of the regions under their control. The honest and efficient governments run by early Muslim rulers combined with the message of a powerful faith to enable the establishment of a civilization that lasted for centuries.

622-632: Period under Muhammad

In 610, Muhammad started to preach Islam in Mecca, where he was bitterly opposed and persecuted. In 622, he migrated to Medina when persecution reached its height and a plot to murder him was hatched. In Medina, where Muhammad was welcome, he was able to preach without restriction and establish the first Islamic society. During the 10 years that Muhammad spent in Medina, he was able to consolidate his power, take control of Mecca, and spread Islam throughout the Arabian Peninsula, with the exception of a few pockets.

632-661: Period under the four caliphs

After Muhammad's death, the Islamic state had four leaders from 632 to 661. They carried the title "caliph," which means "successor." The four caliphs were:

- Abu Bakr from 632 to 634
- Umar ibn al-Khattab from 634 to 644
- Uthman ibn Affan from 644 to 656
- Ali ibn Abu Talib from 656 to 661

Abu Bakr, a very close companion of Muhammad, ruled for only two years. A simple and religious man, he was a highly capable and strong leader. Under his leadership, the Islamic Empire began to expand outside the Arabian Peninsula. When his forces headed into Syria and Iraq, they faced powerful empires, including the Byzantine Empire.

Abu Bakr appointed Umar as the second caliph. During his rule, Syria, Jerusalem, Iran (Persia), Iraq, and Egypt came under the Islamic Empire. After Umar's murder in 644, Uthman and Ali contested the caliphate. Uthman won, but he turned out to be a weak ruler who could not resist the influence of his relatives. A discontented group killed him in 656. During his rule, Islam reached Tunisia and extended further to the east.

Ali became the fourth caliph during whose rule serious internal issues arose. The relatives of Uthman, the third caliph, were upset with Ali because he could not bring to justice those who had killed Uthman. Ali's caliphate ended in 661 when he too was murdered.

661-750: Period under the Ummayyad dynasty

After Ali's assassination the caliphate was taken over by his rival, Muawiyah, the governor of Syria, who established the Ummayyad dynasty. The Ummayyads believed in succession based on inheritance, which was in conflict with the established Islamic practice of electing caliphs. In 661, the Ummayyads moved the caliphate from Medina to Damascus. The shift in power to Damascus had far-reaching implications, the most important being that it shifted the caliph's main focus from religious to secular concerns.

The Ummayyads continued to expand the reach of Islam. They extended the Islamic Empire's influence to the borders of China and Transoxania, an area north of the river Oxus in Central Asia. In 715, Muslims captured the Central Asian cities of Bukhara and Samarkand. They also reached Sind in India and North Africa up to the Atlantic.

In 710, a small Islamic force crossed the eight-mile-wide strait that separates Africa from Spain in a daring raid that led to Spain's first contact with Islam. A year later, a Muslim force of seven thousand invaded Gibraltar. Within the next seven years, almost all of the Iberian Peninsula came under Islamic control. Islamic forces penetrated deep into France but were stopped at the Battle of Tours.

In 747, a rebellion against the Ummayyads in Khorasan, Iran, led to the defeat of its last caliph, Marwan ibn Muhammad, and the end of the Ummayyad dynasty in 750.

750-1258: Period under the Abbassid dynasty

The Abbassids came to power when they overthrew the Ummayyads in 750. They ruled for more than five centuries and made Baghdad the political center of their empire. They distributed power among different ethnic groups and regions and converted the Arab-dominated Islamic Empire into a multinational domain.

Despite the setback in France in 732, when the westward spread of Islam was halted, Islamic influence continued to spread into parts of Asia during the rule of the Abbassids. Islamic forces defeated the Chinese army in Transoxania in 751, which led to the spread of Islam in Central Asia. In the 10th century, Islam spread to Russia. In the 11th century, it spread to the northwestern part of India. The areas of influence under the Abbassids included the Indian subcontinent (India, Pakistan, and Bangladesh), Afghanistan, parts of the Soviet Union, Malaysia, Indonesia, Philippines, China, and Africa.

The Crusades, a set of military expeditions by European Christians between the 11th and 13th centuries to recover the Holy Land from the

Muslims, weakened the Islamic Empire. Also, with the passage of time, decentralization initiated by the Abbassids led to the weakening of their power. Many provinces were minimally controlled and some, such as the Fatimids of Egypt, became independent. The Abbassid dynasty finally came to an end in 1258 when the Mongols captured Baghdad and executed the last Abbassid caliph.

750-950: Golden Age of Islam

When the Ummayyad dynasty was overthrown in 750, its sole surviving member, Abd al-Rahman ibn Muawiyah, escaped to Spain, where he restarted the Ummayyad dynasty and caliphate in 756. It was the beginning of a great Islamic civilization, one of the greatest the world has ever seen. It led to Spain's becoming Europe's center of learning as well as the cultural center of Islam in the West.

The Golden Age of Islam lasted about two hundred years. During that period, the Islamic Empire covered Spain, North Africa, Egypt, Iraq, Iran, Syria, Palestine, and parts of Turkey. The Golden Age of Islam was characterized by:

- Flourishing of science, chemistry, astronomy, technology, mathematics, literature, philosophy, and the arts
- Development of the astrolabe, an instrument for measuring the altitude of heavenly bodies and determining their positions and movements, and the building of the world's first observatory
- Contributions to medicine, including drugs and expansion of knowledge of anatomy, dissection, and blood circulation
- Introduction of Arabic numerals, which influenced the development of algebra
- Advances in agriculture, including underground canals, networks of wells, waterwheels, and livestock improvement
- Development of the art of making paper

- Establishment of a paper mill in Baghdad, which had a significant influence on education and made possible the widespread distribution of books
- Development of Arabic into the language of international scholarship
- Massive efforts to translate scientific manuscripts into Arabic
- Spreading of libraries

Many advances made during the Golden Age laid the groundwork for developments that led to the Renaissance in Europe. The peak of the Golden Age is considered to have occurred during the rule of al-Mamun, who died in 833.

ISLAM'S CONTRIBUTION AND IMPACT

Dignity

For centuries, Islam has helped millions of men and women lead their lives with dignity despite difficult and deprived living conditions. It provided them peace of mind even when faced with a future that held little or no hope. It also provided an objective for their lives—achieving a far better life in the hereafter. It was an objective they believed could be achieved despite the hopeless circumstances in which they lived.

Islamic civilization

The Islamic civilization was one of the greatest contributions made by Islam. Its influence and benefits were not limited to Muslims. Its impact was felt throughout the known world. The Islamic civilization brought into its fold people of diverse ethnic and religious backgrounds. They contributed to the advancement of knowledge and developments in various fields such as science, mathematics, and medicine. In particular, scientific development in the Islamic world, from the 8th to the 11th century, became the basis of knowledge in the world.

Global influence

The influence of Islam and the Islamic civilization was felt in vast areas that covered Asia, Europe, and Africa. The spread of Islam accelerated a few years after Muhammad's death. It included people of every ethnic group it contacted, including Arabs, Persians, Turks, Egyptians, Europeans, Russians, Chinese, Mongols, and Indonesians. Every area that converted to Islam during that period contributed to the Islamic civilization. A primary reason that the Islamic civilization was able to develop and flower was its message of brotherhood and its ability to absorb and incorporate from:

- Earlier civilizations
- Countries where it spread
- Various ethnic and racial groups
- Various languages

Nurturer of knowledge during the Dark Ages

The Dark Ages in Europe started in the late 5th century and lasted for approximately six hundred years. During its peak, the Islamic civilization was in full bloom. It became the center of knowledge and established high standards in mathematics, science, astronomy, medicine, and other fields. While Europe remained stagnant, Islamic scholars, scientists, and mathematicians made major advances. European scholars who flocked to the Islamic civilization's libraries and universities transferred the knowledge they gained back to Europe. The roots of the subsequent Renaissance, which occurred between the 14th and 16th centuries, are attributed to contact with the Islamic civilization that kept scholarship alive through the Dark Ages.

Areas of excellence and contribution

Contributions that can be attributed to the Islamic civilization extend to many areas, including:
- Astronomy: Accomplishments included a precise solar calendar (Jilali); discovery of new stars; development of observatories, the quadrant, and the astrolabe (which led to advances in ocean navigation).
- Geography and history: Developed world maps, led explorations as ship navigators, and wrote comprehensive world histories and geographies.
- Medicine: Organized hospitals (including mobile); areas of development included anatomy and physiology, hygiene, surgery and surgical instruments, and pharmacology.
- Mathematics: Organized numbers into the decimal system; invented algebra and trigonometry.
- Physics: Demonstrated the theory of parallels.

Another major Muslim achievement was the writing of books and papers. Razi wrote approximately two hundred books while Thabit ibn Qurra had more than seventy original works to his credit. ibn Sina's medical book, al-Qanun, was used as a standard textbook for seven hundred years in many Asian countries as well as in Europe. Muslims also translated thousands of books into Arabic, which they used to enrich their libraries and draw readers from all over Europe.

The Islamic civilization produced a number of world-renowned scholars, scientists, and physicians. Some of the most prominent were:
- Umar Khayyam (astronomer)
- ibn Batuta (world traveler, also known as Muslim Marco Polo)
- ibn Khaldun (historian and geography writer)
- al-Khawarizmi, al-Biruni, Banu Musa, and al-Hasan (mathematicians)

- ibn Sina and al-Razi (physicians)
- Khalaf Abul-Qasim al-Zahrawi (surgeon)
- ibn al-Haytham (physicist)

CHAPTER 2

DECLINE OF ISLAMIC CIVILIZATION AND PRESENT STATUS

DECLINE OF MUSLIM DYNASTIES AND EMPIRES

How the decline occurred

The Islamic civilization reached its peak during the Golden Age of Islam from 750 to 950, then began a slow decline that continued for many centuries. A variety of factors led to the decline and ultimate end of the Islamic Empire.

End of the Abbassid dynasty

During the rule of Harun al-Rashid, which lasted from 786 to 809, parts of North Africa broke away from Abbassid control. During the reign of al-Mamun, recognized as the greatest Abbassid, other provinces also broke free. The decline worsened following his death in 833. In the next four centuries, a number of provinces broke away. During the 11th and 12th centuries, the Crusades weakened the Islamic Empire. The Crusades ended in 1187 after Salahuddin Ayyubi, of Egypt, defeated the Crusaders and conquered Jerusalem—but not before considerable damage had been done.

The Abbassid rule came to an end in 1258 when the Mongols sacked Baghdad. This led to the division of the Islamic Empire into three parts dominated by the Mongols, Arabs, and Turks (Seljuk and Mamluk):

- Central Asia (under Mongols)
- North Africa (under Arabs)
- West (under Turks)

Fatimid dynasty

The Fatimid dynasty, which belonged to the Shia sect of Islam, was founded in the 10th century when the central control of the Abbassids declined. The Fatimids established a caliphate in North Africa and extended its influence to the Red Sea, Yemen, and parts of Syria and Palestine. However, the Fatimids never realized their desire to control the Arabian Peninsula and Iraq—areas considered to be the center of the Islamic world. The Fatimid dynasty lasted till the 12th century.

Seljuk Turks

The Seljuk Turks, originally from an area near the Aral Sea, were tough fighters who began to play a role in the Middle East in the 11th century. They controlled a state, nominally under the Abbassid caliphs, that extended from Central Asia to Asia Minor. The area under their control included all of the Middle East, part of the Arabian Peninsula, Kyrgystan, Uzbekistan, Turkmenistan, Kazakhstan, and Turkey. It disintegrated following internal conflicts and power struggles that started in 1092. The Seljuk's rule lasted till the 13th century.

Mongols

The Mongols, led by Genghis Khan, became a very powerful force in the 13th century. They overran China, Russia, Central Asia, Central Europe, Caucuses, and Northern Iran. In 1258, led by Halagu Khan, the grandson of Genghis Khan, the Mongols attacked Baghdad and ended the rule of the Abbassids. The Mongol takeover of Baghdad led to the killing of most of the city's one hundred thousand inhabitants.

The Mongol attack devastated the Islamic heartland and led to its decline. In a short time, the Mongols shattered a legacy of five hundred years. They destroyed irrigation systems, libraries, and cultural and other achievements of the Golden Age. The Mongols culminated their destruction by killing scientists and scholars. Their onslaught ended in 1260 when they moved against Egypt and were defeated by the Mamluks.

After coming into contact with Islam, Mongols began to embrace the religion. They recognized Islam as the official religion at the start of the 14th century. Tamerlane, a descendent of Genghis Khan, led the Mongols' second major attack in the 14th century. His forces swept across Central Asia, Iraq, Iraq, Syria, and India. His vast empire extended from Kiev in Russia to Western China. However, Tamerlane's empire disintegrated following his death because he failed to install stable governments in captured territories.

Fall of Spain in 1492

The first resistance to Muslim rule in Spain, which came in the 11th century as they weakened due to internal dissension, was put down with the help of North African Berbers. However, lack of unity continued to plague Muslims despite the growth of external threats. On the other hand, Christian kingdoms continued to form alliances and started to present a real threat. The result was that Muslims began to be pushed steadily back to the south. By the 13th century, they had been forced to retreat to a few scattered kingdoms in southern Spain.

In 1469, Ferdinand and Isabella, known as the Catholic kings, married and joined forces. Helped by the split in the ranks of the Muslims, they captured Granada, the last Muslim kingdom, in 1492. Muslims lived in Spain until the Inquisition led to the loss of their rights and, with life becoming very difficult, they began to emigrate. The remaining Muslims were forced out of Spain at the beginning of the 17th century.

End of the Safavid Empire

The Safavid Empire was founded in Persia (Iran) in 1501 and lasted till 1722. It was a Shiite empire that did not have good relations with its Sunni neighbors due to sectarian differences. It was the second Islamic Empire to form after the Ottoman Empire. Invading Afghans ended the Safavid Empire in 1722.

End of the Mughal Empire

A number of Muslim dynasties ruled over India following its first invasion from the northwest by Mahmud Ghazni in the year 1000. They included the Slave, Khilji, Tughlaq, Sayyid, and Lodhi dynasties.

In 1526, Babar, a descendant of Genghis Khan, defeated Ibrahim Lodhi, India's ruler. Following his victory at Panipat, he started the Mughal Empire, which ruled the Indian subcontinent for more than three hundred years. While the first six Mughal kings were powerful, subsequent rulers were weak and ineffectual. Their power continued to weaken as the British colonized India. In 1857, following a revolt against the British, the last Mughal ruler was deposed and exiled to Burma.

End of the Ottoman Empire

The Turk-dominated Ottoman Empire, founded by Osman, came to power in 1299. In the 14th century it captured most of Asia Minor from the Byzantine Empire. In 1453, it took Constantinople and made it the capital, renaming it Istanbul. The Ottomans continued to expand to:

- Southeast Europe: Greece, Serbia, Bosnia, and Hungary
- East and South: Iraq, Arabia, and Egypt

The Ottomans reached their peak under Suleiman the Magnificent, who died in 1566. They reached Poland but their second attempt to take Vienna failed in 1683. That was the turning point for the Ottomans. They were driven out of Poland in the 17th century and from the Balkans and Greece in the 19th century. The Ottoman Empire broke up after the end of World War I, in which it was allied with Germany. In 1922, the Turkish Sultanate was abolished followed by the Turkish caliphate in 1924. In 1928, Turkey was declared a secular state.

MODERN WORLD EVENTS AND DEVELOPMENTS

Colonial subjugation

In 1798, Napoleon Bonaparte invaded Egypt, which was a part of the Ottoman Empire. The invasion spearheaded the way for European intervention in the Middle East. Subsequent events included:
- 1830: France occupied Algeria
- 1839: Britain occupied Aden
- 1853: Arab sheikhdoms of the Persian Gulf recognized Britain as the dominant power in the Gulf
- 1857: British crown took over India
- 1881: France occupied Tunisia
- 1882: Britain occupied Egypt
- 1906: Morocco-Algeciras conference formalized division between France and Spain
- 1911: Italy occupied Libya

The British incited Arabs to revolt against the Ottoman Empire during World War I by promising aid and independence. The Arabs managed to divert the Turks, who were Germany's allies, and contributed to the Allied victory. However, Britain and France secretly agreed to partition the Arab areas of the Ottoman Empire. The result was that France occupied Syria and Lebanon while Britain took over Palestine, Iraq, and TransJordan.

Colonial expansion by the Europeans, at its peak in the 19th century, led to loss of freedom for large parts of the Islamic world and was a turning point in Muslim history. Countries not directly subjugated were either under European influence or under threat of being overcome by it. The most important aspect of colonial subjugation for Muslims was that it led to the undermining of traditional Islamic systems of governance, social structure, and education.

Major 20th-century developments

Balfour Declaration sows seeds of future conflict

In 1896, Theodor Herzl, a Hungarian Jew and the founder of Zionism, wrote a paper that proposed the establishment of a Jewish state in Argentina or Palestine. In 1917, when Arabs constituted 92 percent of Palestine's population, the British issued the Balfour Declaration that promised support for a "national home for the Jewish people" in Palestine. Jewish leaders considered this to mean support for a Jewish country. However, historians disagree over its interpretation. Some do not believe the declaration supported the creation of a Jewish state because it had no mention of the word *state*.

The result of the Balfour Declaration was an increase in Jewish immigration to Palestine. The influx rose considerably after Hitler came to power and started to persecute Jews. The increase in Jewish immigration caused serious conflicts with the British, who tried to control it, and with the local Arab population. In 1947, the United Nations (UN) decided to partition Palestine into Arab and Jewish states. After Israel declared its independence in 1948, war broke out when Arab neighbors attacked the newly formed Jewish state. The Arabs were defeated and millions of Palestinians became refugees.

There were three subsequent wars between the Arabs and the Israelis: in 1956, 1967, and 1973. The Arabs lost each time. In spite of many attempts since the first war, permanent peace has remained elusive and, to this day, Arabs and Israelis remain enemies in a war with new battlegrounds in the towns and streets of Palestine and Israel.

Islamic states are formed

In the 20th century, European powers started to free their Asian and African colonies, which led to independence for many countries that had large or predominant Muslim populations. These included:
- Africa: Egypt, Sudan, Tunisia, Morocco, Niger, Chad, Somalia, Niger, Mali, and Senegal
- Asia: Indonesia, Pakistan, Bangladesh, Malaysia, and Brunei
- Middle East: Saudi Arabia, Iraq, Syria, The Yemens, TransJordan, Libya, Kuwait, Lebanon, and the United Arab Emirates

Most of the colonies became free through a peaceful process although some achieved independence through armed revolt, including Algeria, Libya, Morocco, Tunisia, and Indonesia. The Algerian revolt against France was brutal and bloody. In 1947, Pakistan was created after a peaceful movement when India was partitioned into India and Pakistan. However, the partition led to cross-migration of Hindus and Muslims, between India and Pakistan, as well as widespread Hindu-Muslim riots. Millions were killed during the migration and riots that engulfed the subcontinent.

ISLAM IN TODAY'S WORLD

Widespread underdeveloped Muslim societies

Muslim countries at this time are, by and large, relatively underdeveloped. The reasons for the current state of Muslim societies include:
- Wrong priorities
- Mass illiteracy and lack of education
- Adopting harmful customs and practices
- Religious and political leaders who reach their positions due to hereditary and social factors rather than knowledge, character, and ability
- Paying lip service to, but not following, the teachings and principles of Islam that they claim to uphold
- Personal characteristics that do not meet the high standards set by Islam
- Paying attention to Islamic acts of worship, such as praying and fasting, but failing to implement its high values in society
- Paying lip service to, but not implementing, the rights enjoined by Islam such as:
  - Democracy
  - Equality and justice
  - Fundamental and human rights
  - Women's rights
  - Succession rights for property
  - Freedom to choose mates

Population

Various sources provide different estimates for the worldwide population of Muslims. According to the *World Christian Encyclopedia*, there are 1.21 billion Muslims, representing 20 percent of the world population. It is the second largest religion after Christianity, which is claimed by 33 percent of the population. Islam is estimated to be growing at an annual rate of 2.9 percent while Christianity is growing at 2.3 percent. If present trends continue, Islam will become the largest religion before the end of the 21st century.

Areas of concentration

The followers of Islam are found in all parts of the world. About 47 percent of Muslims live in four southern and southeastern Asian countries: Indonesia, Pakistan, India, and Bangladesh. The countries with the largest numbers of Muslims are:
- Indonesia: 201 million
- Pakistan: 140 million
- India: 123 million
- Bangladesh: 109 million
- Turkey: 66 million
- Egypt: 65 million
- Nigeria: 63 million

Additional facts about the distribution of Muslims early in the 21st century are:
- Muslims are in a majority in 54 countries
- Even though Islam began in the Middle East, Arabs account for only 22 percent of Muslims
- 30 percent of Muslims live in the Indian subcontinent (India, Pakistan, and Bangladesh)
- Even though India has the third largest Muslim population in the world, it forms only 12 percent of India's huge population
- Muslims are in a majority in two European countries—Bosnia and Albania
- Six million Muslims live in the United States
- Five million Muslims live in France, Germany, and the United Kingdom

Ethnic diversity

Since Islam taught that ethnicity is an irrelevant factor for those coming into its fold, it appealed broadly across continents and ethnic divisions. Consequently, followers of Islam include practically every ethnic group. Large numbers of Muslims can be found among Asians, Europeans, Africans, Persians, Arabs, Chinese, Russians, Malays, Africans, Mongols, and other ethnic groups.

Cultural diversity

The geographic range of Muslims has resulted in broad cultural diversity, which is reflected in languages, attire, food, customs, and traditions. Muslims living in each area have distinctive characteristics that, in many cases, seem odd to Muslims living in other areas. This diversity has also resulted in local traditions and customs seeping into the practice of Islam even though, at times, such practices are contradictory and violate Islamic teachings. In general, no local practice is unacceptable to Islam so long as it does not violate Islamic principles.

Political diversity

There is no central Islamic religious or political authority acknowledged by Muslims. Mecca and Medina are considered to be religious, not political, centers. Political leadership of Muslims varies from country to country and region to region. Present-day rule in Muslim countries includes monarchies, democracies, and military dictatorships. Political diversity includes rule by Sharia, or Islamic law, as well as presidential and parliamentary styles of government.

Myth of unity and brotherhood

Islam teaches that Muslims must be united in a single brotherhood, or Ummah, by a common faith. On a personal level, Muslims consider Muslims all over the world as their brothers and sisters. They sympathize with them during difficult times and crises. However, political unity has been a mirage even though there is plenty of lip service paid to it. Politically, at this time, Muslims are even more disunited than they have been for most of their history.

Common misconception about Arabs and Muslims

Islam started in an Arab country and spread across many diverse countries all over the world. Over time, Arabs became a minority within Muslims and, at this time, the majority of Muslims are non-Arabs, a fact unknown to many non-Muslims who mistakenly think all Muslims are Arabs. An Arab can be a Muslim, a Christian, or a Jew. All Muslims are not Arabs and all Arabs are not Muslims. Only 22 percent of Muslims are Arabs. In other words, 78 percent of Muslims are non-Arabs. In the 22 Arab countries, about 7 percent of the population is non-Muslim.

ISLAM IN AMERICA

History of Islam in America

The first Muslims to arrive in America were African slaves. Due to their lack of freedom as well as unstable social and family conditions, they were unable to maintain their identity and, over time, Islam was lost by their offspring. Arabs started to emigrate at the beginning of the 20th century, followed by European Muslims, although the number of immigrants was insignificant during the first half of the 20th century.

In the 1960s and 1970s, the Black Muslim movement attracted many African-Americans. However, many converts turned away from the Black Muslim religion when they realized that it did not represent true Islam and, in fact, preached the opposite of what orthodox Islam stood for. The first important defector was Malcolm X, who joined mainstream Islam after he broke away. Following his lead, over time a large number of African-Americans defected from the Black Muslim movement. A sizeable number of African-Americans also converted directly from Christianity to Islam.

In the 1970s and 1980s, a large number of Muslim immigrants arrived in America. They were the dependents and relatives of the tens of thousands of Muslim students who came to America from all parts of the world to obtain an education but never returned after completing their studies.

Population

Islam is the fastest growing religion in America. At this time, it is estimated that there are six million Muslims in the United States. Some estimates run as high as eight million. Assuming six million is correct, the American Muslim population is on a par with the American Jewish population. About one million Muslims are estimated to be African-Americans though some figures run as high as two million. Muslims outnumber Presbyterians, Lutherans, and Episcopalians. According to a Zogby International poll commissioned by the American Muslim Council in August 2000:

- The percentage of American Muslims by origin is:
  - 26.2 percent Middle East Arab
  - 24.7 percent South Asia
  - 23.8 percent African-American
  - 11.6 percent Other
  - 10.3 percent Middle East non-Arab
  - 3.4 percent East Asia
- 22.4 percent of American Muslims were born in the U.S.

Dynamic community

Muslims in America are found in all walks of life. A very high percentage of Muslims are professionals such as doctors, engineers, and

scientists. More than 61 percent of American Muslims are college graduates, compared to 43.7 percent of all Americans. Muslims can be found in every state. Their distribution is[1]:
- East: 32.2 percent
- South: 25.3 percent
- Central/Great Lakes: 24.3 percent
- West: 18.2 percent

There are hundreds of part-time Islamic schools, a few colleges, and more than two thousand mosques patronized by American Muslims. Thousands of community centers, which provide cultural and social programs, have been established all over the country.

---

1. Source: Zogby International, August 2000.

CHAPTER 3

DEFINING EVENTS AND HOW MUSLIMS VIEW THEM

HISTORICAL EVENTS

Introduction

After Muhammad formalized Islam as a religion and established the first Islamic society and state, the religion had a meteoric rise that led to the establishment of the Islamic civilization. After a glorious era, it started a descent that continues today. Though there have been periodic attempts at revival, Muslims have had, at best, limited success. The events of the last 14 centuries, since Muhammad introduced Islam, have shaped the way Muslims think and how they react to what is happening around them and in the rest of the world.

The following sections describe how Muslims perceive some of the major events that have impacted them and influenced their thinking and behavior.

Decline of Islamic civilization after its Golden Age

The Islamic civilization was at its zenith during the Golden Age, from 750 to 950, which is the benchmark against which Muslims compare their current condition. Since that time, except for brief periods, the political and economic condition of Muslims has deteriorated in tandem with the decline of the Islamic civilization. Despite the tremendous deterioration that has already taken place, their decline continues except in isolated pockets. Most Muslims perceive their current condition as being the worst ever in the nearly fourteen-hundred year history of Islam.

Crusades

Christians launched a number of Crusades against the Muslims. Pope Urban II initiated the first Crusade in 1095 with the objective of regaining Jerusalem from the Muslims. He succeeded in 1099. When the Crusaders captured Jerusalem after a five-week siege, they massacred the city's Jews and Muslims. The second Crusade took place in 1147, following the 1144 Muslim capture of Edessa, one of four Crusader states along the Palestinian and Syrian coast. The Crusades effectively ended in 1187 when Salahuddin Ayyubi defeated the Crusaders and recaptured Jerusalem. The third Crusade was initiated a year after Salahuddin's victory. In the following century, Europeans initiated a number of expeditions against the Muslims but failed to realize their objectives. Muslims perceive the Crusades as the start of the Western civilization's systematic effort against Islam that, under various guises, still continues.

Failed Turkish siege of Vienna

The Ottoman Empire's first attempt to conquer Vienna during its expansionist drive, which failed, took place in 1529. In 1683, the Turks tried again. The second siege also failed. One of the primary reasons for the defeat of the Turks was the advanced firepower used against them by the Europeans. In the three centuries since then, Muslims have been on the defensive, especially since the establishment of European colonial empires in Africa and Asia.

End of the Ottoman Empire

The Ottoman Empire came to an end in 1922 when Mustafa Kemal Ataturk, an army officer, took control of Turkey. He declared it a republic and deposed the sultan. In 1924, world Muslims lost the symbolic head of the Islamic community when the caliphate was abolished by Ataturk.

Kemal Ataturk implemented major changes in Turkey and made it a secular state. He was the only leader in the first half of the 20th century who led any serious attempt to modernize and uplift Muslims from their abject condition. Ataturk's attempt to leapfrog his country into modernism and westernize it was not appreciated by Muslims throughout the world. Instead of performing self-evaluation and addressing the problems that had led to their decline, they lamented the loss of a figurehead leader, the caliph.

Revival and reform movements

The condition of Muslims in the past two centuries led to the development of many revival and reform movements in Muslim countries. These movements had different objectives, including educational and social reform, economic uplift, and religious revival.

One of the reform movements with significant, worldwide impact is the religious movement started by Abd al-Wahhab, an Arabian who died in 1792. His reform effort led to the development of the puritanical Wahhabi Islamic sect. The followers of Abd al-Wahhab supported the founder of the present Saudi dynasty, Muhammad ibn al-Saud, and helped him come to power. Since then, the Saudi royal family has let the ideology of the Wahhabis govern their country. They have kept the

Wahhabis happy by adhering to religious extremism and exporting their religious beliefs. As part of their effort to project a religiously correct image to their domestic religious extremists, Saudi rulers have patronized extremist schools and religious organizations outside their country. They include many of the madrassas that have been producing religious zealots with minimal knowledge and understanding of the secular world.

Egypt has seen the growth of many religious movements including the Muslim Brotherhood (Ikhwan al-Muslimeen), which has branches in many countries, and the Egyptian Islamic Jehad. For many of these movements, the goal has been to slow or prevent Westernization and to establish an Islamic society. Osama bin Laden's right-hand man, Dr. Ayman al-Zawahri, headed one of the factions of the Islamic Jehad, which has been active in Egypt since the late 1970s. Its goal is to overthrow the Egyptian government and replace it with an Islamic state.

End of the colonial era

After World War I, European countries started to think seriously about granting independence to colonies in Asia and Africa. In 1922, Egypt became nominally independent from Britain while Iraq became independent in 1932. In 1946, Jordan, Lebanon, and Syria were granted independence by Britain and France. Muslim countries that became independent after World War II include Indonesia, Pakistan, Libya, Sudan, Tunisia, Morocco, Malaysia, Nigeria, Senegal, Somalia, Kuwait, Algeria, and the United Arab Emirates.

The boundaries of many of the new countries in the Middle East, including Jordan and Iraq, were arbitrarily delineated. Decisions were based on political payoffs to Arab royal families, in return for their military help against the Ottoman Empire and others who fought the British and their Allies during World War II, or for other subjective considerations.

Drawing national boundaries without considering historical and ethnic backgrounds caused many problems for the leaders of the newly independent nations. The machinations of leaders in neighboring countries forced them to focus on survival and building up armies instead of economic development. Examples of these include India, Pakistan, Syria, Lebanon, Iraq, and Kuwait. Instead of moving forward, many of these countries ended up in worse condition than before independence. Generations were denied basic education as well as health and social services. Faulty demarcation decisions also laid seeds of trouble, for years and decades to come, as has been clearly demonstrated in the Iraq-Kuwait crisis of 1990 and the festering Palestine problem.

Saudi Arabia comes under the Saud family rule

In 1902, Abdul Aziz al-Saud captured Riyadh and started the modern Saud dynasty in Arabia. He consolidated the oil-rich country and helped the British defeat the Ottoman Empire, which had ruled his country. Following the end of Turkish rule, the country was renamed Saudi Arabia in 1933. An overwhelming majority of Muslims believe that the Arab revolt against the Turks was a conspiracy by the West with two objectives:
- Weaken Muslims by making them fight each other
- Control Saudi Arabia's vast oil resources

EVENTS AFTER 1947

Partition of India

Before the British left India in 1947, they partitioned the colony into two countries: India and Pakistan. Pakistan became the first officially declared Islamic country of the modern era. India's religion-based partition led to mass migrations. Hindus migrated from Muslim-majority areas to India, while Muslims migrated to Pakistan from Hindu-majority areas. Although millions migrated across the boundaries, and more than three million Hindus and Muslims were killed during their migration attempt, many chose to remain behind.

Millions of poor and illiterate Muslims stayed in India while most educated Muslims and leaders migrated to Pakistan. Consequently, Muslims in Hindu-majority India were subjected to blatant discrimination and, being leaderless, were unable to cope. The condition of Indian Muslims, who number 123 million, has gone from bad to worse in the past five decades. Most live in ghettos and are periodically attacked by armed Hindus, often actively aided by the police. Since 1947, hundreds of thousands of Muslims have been killed in riots and pogroms. In just one month, March 2002, more than eight hundred Muslims were killed in a single Indian state, Gujarat. Some estimates put the number of Muslims killed in the riots at over two thousand.

In 1992, the well-known Babri mosque was demolished by thousands of ultranationalist Hindus in a well-planned attack. Despite months of warning signs and openly aired threats, the government and police did nothing to prevent the attack. Indian Muslims perceived that event as the worst symbolic act against them, which led to riots that killed thousands of Muslims and destroyed thousands of their businesses and homes.

Kashmir

When India was partitioned in 1947, Kashmir was expected to become a part of Pakistan based on partition rules. However, the Hindu ruler of Kashmir, which was overwhelmingly Muslim, opted to join India against the wishes of the Kashmiris. The people revolted, forcing him to ask India for military help, which led to war between India and Pakistan. Intervention by the United Nations led to a cease-fire in January 1949 and India promised to hold a plebiscite, as UN resolutions demanded, to determine the wishes of the Kashmiris. However, India used the cease-fire to buy time and consolidate its physical hold on Kashmir.

Pakistan joined the American-sponsored SEATO (Southeast Asia Treaty Organization) anti-communist defense treaty in 1954, which was followed by its membership in the CENTO (Central Treaty Organization) treaty. Those actions, which took place at the height of the Cold War, provided India an opportunity to enlist the help of the Soviet Union, which had started to view Pakistan as an unfriendly nation because of its military ties with America. Subsequently, every United Nations resolution on Kashmir that referred to the Kashmiris' right of self-determination, and India's prior commitments to the United Nations and the Kashmiris, was vetoed by the Soviet Union.

Since 1947, Kashmir has been a festering problem. In 1989, it exploded into an armed rebellion that is still continuing. More than seven hundred thousand Indian army troops and paramilitary personnel have tried unsuccessfully to suppress a population of only seven million. An estimated sixty thousand Kashmiris have been killed since 1989, the equivalent of more than two million people being killed in the United States. In perspective, fifty-four thousand American lives were lost in the Vietnam War.

Muslims view the Kashmir issue as a classic example of Western and American indifference to Muslim suffering and issues. While America went to extreme lengths to impose and force implementation of UN resolutions on Iraq, it has never required India to fulfill its UN obligations. America has also ignored India's gross violations of human rights in Kashmir, which have been well documented by various human rights groups including Amnesty International and Human Rights Watch. Violations include thousands of cases of torture, deaths in custody, extrajudicial executions, "disappearances," and 6,300 reported rapes. According to Muslims, America applies a different set of rules to India for two main reasons. First, it is a large country that benefits American business interests. Second, it is strategically positioned against China, which America considers to be a potential long-term threat.

Palestine

Israel was carved out of Palestine in 1948 to provide a homeland for the Jews. Since then, Israelis have defeated Arabs in four wars. During the 1967 war, Israel expanded its boundaries considerably and occupied the West Bank, Gaza Strip, and East Jerusalem. Since 1948, Israeli society has prospered economically while most Palestinians have been living in ghetto-like conditions, either within Palestine or as refugees in other countries, with no hope for the future.

Muslims throughout the world view the Palestine problem as a religious issue due to the Israeli occupation of Jerusalem, where the al-Aqsa mosque is located. al-Aqsa is revered as the third most important Islamic religious site after Mecca and Medina. Muslims believe that Jews want to take over the al-Aqsa mosque, which is adjacent to the holiest site for Jews, the Wailing Wall. The basis for such thinking is the attempt by an Australian tourist to burn down the mosque in 1969, two years after Israel occupied East Jerusalem.

Muslims are incensed at the Israeli occupation of Palestine and the way in which the Palestinians have been oppressed and denied freedom since 1967. Most consider the oppression of the Palestinians as equivalent to the oppression of Muslims.

Overthrow of Mossadegh in Iran

In 1951, Dr. Mohammad Mossadegh, the nationalist prime minister of Iran, nationalized the oil industry and formed a national oil company in order to control his country's oil resources. The nationalization caused a financial loss to the British government because it owned a significant part of the Anglo-Iranian Oil Company, which had been put out of business by Mossadegh's action. It is interesting to note that the Anglo-Iranian Oil Company had been paying far more to the British government in taxes than it had been paying to the Iranians. The British retaliated by imposing a worldwide embargo on Iranian oil, freezing Iran's sterling assets, and banning the export of goods to Iran.

The Iranian monarch, the Shah of Iran, opposed Mossadegh. In 1952, Mossadegh resigned after a power struggle with the Shah. However, street rioting forced the Shah to reinstate him. The British, who could not come to terms with their loss, proposed to the Americans that they jointly overthrow Mossadegh. The Americans responded favorably because they had started to get worried about the Tudeh (Communist) party's role and the potential for the Russians to get a foothold in Iran at the height of the Cold War. A British-American plan, code named Operation Ajax, was developed to overthrow Mossadegh.

The CIA and MI6, the British Secret Intelligence Service, jointly executed Operation Ajax in August 1953. Initially, the coup failed and the Shah was forced to flee to Italy. However, the plan ultimately succeeded, Mossadegh was overthrown, and the Shah returned to power. Subsequently, a consortium of American, British, French, and Dutch oil companies reached a deal with Iran to operate its oil facilities. The deal was based on equal sharing of profits between the consortium and Iran.

Arab defeats in four wars

In the first Arab-Israeli war, which took place when Israel was created in 1948, the Israelis defeated the combined armies of its Arab neighbors. In 1956, Egypt nationalized the Suez Canal. Its action led to military intervention by the British and French, who bombed Egyptian airfields and took over the canal, while the Israeli army moved into the Sinai and defeated the Egyptian army.

In the Six-Day War of 1967, the Israelis again defeated the Arabs including the Syrians, Jordanians, and Egyptians. In that war, Israel reached the height of its expansion and occupied the Golan Heights, the West Bank, Gaza Strip, and Jerusalem's Old City.

In 1973, Egypt launched a surprise attack that drove the Israelis back from the Suez Canal. The Israelis mounted a successful counterattack and pushed the Egyptians back to the canal. When a cease-fire was implemented, the Egyptian army was in complete disarray.

The four successive defeats have resulted in deep humiliation for Muslims. It has introduced a profound sense of frustration and helplessness. They attribute the defeats to superior Israeli technology and military support provided by the United States. The defeats have reinforced the Muslim perception that they are being targeted and victimized.

1973 oil embargo

The 1973 Arab-Israeli war led to the Arabs imposing an oil embargo on Western countries. For the first time in modern history, the Arabs were united. Along with the oil embargo, they raised the price of oil to astronomical levels that caused gasoline shortages in America. The temporary success of the embargo, which disrupted day-to-day life in the West, gave Arabs and Muslims their first sense of power in modern times. However, that was a temporary phenomenon as the price of oil collapsed after remaining high for only a few years. The loss of pricing power and ability to control the oil market has led to a widespread view among Muslims that American oil companies and Western governments have conspired to hurt oil-rich Muslim countries economically.

Soviet Union's defeat in Afghanistan

The introduction of reforms by Afghanistan's communist government, which came to power in 1978, was bitterly opposed by ultraconservative Afghans. In 1979, when it appeared that the wobbly government might fall, the Soviet Union sent military forces into Afghanistan to help prop up the communists. The move backfired when Afghans reacted by starting a guerrilla campaign. Americans, sensing an opportunity to weaken the Soviet Union through a proxy war, helped the Afghan rebels. Afghan guerillas were provided billions of dollars in aid and state-of-the-art weapons, such as the deadly Stinger missile, which helped turn the tide of war.

Muslim men from throughout the world participated in the Afghanistan war against the Soviets. They responded to the first and only widespread call in modern history for participation in the extreme form of jehad, which requires the taking up of arms in the defense of Islam or Muslims. After a decade of war, the Soviet army was forced to withdraw in 1989. The victory by the mujahideen against a superpower was a great morale booster for Muslims throughout the world. However, the victory was hollow because Afghans became embroiled in a civil war due to political and tribal rivalries. The civil war caused far more death and destruction than the Soviet army had inflicted.

Breakup of the Soviet Union

The breakup of the Soviet Union after the fall of communism in 1989 changed the political map of Central Asia. It led to the creation of many new countries with Muslim majority populations: Kazakhstan, Kyrgyzstan, Tajikistan, Turkmenistan, and Uzbekistan. With the lifting of religious restrictions, there was a resurgence of Islam in those countries. The new political setup also led to closer ties and economic relations with neighboring countries to the south, all Islamic.

Another fallout from the breakup was the revolt in Chechnya, a predominantly Muslim Russian republic. Russia refused to grant it independence, and the result has been a protracted and bloody conflict that started in 1994 and still continues. Muslims point to Chechnya as an example, in addition to Bosnia, of their being suppressed ruthlessly without any meaningful protest by Western powers.

Gulf War

In 1990, Iraq captured Kuwait in a lightning attack. The United States reacted to the invasion by organizing a coalition of 28 countries with the objective of driving Iraq out of Kuwait. Many Muslim countries joined the coalition, some out of fear, including Saudi Arabia, Pakistan, and Egypt. In 1991, the coalition forces attacked Iraqi occupation forces in Kuwait. The highly acclaimed Iraqi army, which was expected to put up stiff resistance due to its battle experience in the eight-year war with Iran, was routed in less than four days. Many Muslims view its rout as the defeat of a Muslim country rather than the defeat of an aggressor.

Bosnia massacres

The breakup of Yugoslavia led to the creation of new countries such as Serbia, Croatia, and Bosnia. Nationhood was achieved by Bosnia only after one of the bloodiest struggles in the history of Europe. When Bosnia declared its independence, Serbians started the ethnic cleansing of Muslims. Mass executions, burning and pillaging, rape, and other heinous crimes were carried out for more than two years. While the world watched in horror, the West stood frozen. An ineffectual arms embargo stopped weapon supplies to the Bosnians, the victims, but did not block arms supplies to Serbian aggressors.

Muslims all over the world believe that the arms embargo, and the reluctance of the West to get involved for a long time, was driven by its desire to prevent the formation of the first Muslim country in modern Europe. Those who do not subscribe to this view believe that if the victims had been non-Muslims, the reaction by the West would have been swift and completely different.

Beirut, Somalia, and South Lebanon

In 1982, the Israelis invaded Lebanon and occupied South Lebanon. Their objective was to create a buffer zone that would help protect its settlements from armed Hezbollah guerrilla attacks. However, the occupation proved to be costly as the guerillas extracted a heavy toll on Israeli forces. By 2000, Hezbollah's continuing attacks and never-ending Israeli casualties forced Israel to withdraw.

In October 1983, a suicide bomber blew up the United States Marine barracks in Beirut, Lebanon, killing more than two hundred marines. The devastating bombing led to the decision by President Reagan to withdraw American forces from Lebanon.

In 1992, America led an international humanitarian effort to provide aid to Somalia, a Muslim country that had been ravaged by civil war, drought, and famine. However, America quickly pulled out its troops in 1993 after a warlord's deadly attack resulted in the death of 18 American soldiers.

Muslim extremists view these three events as examples of what dedicated Muslims can achieve. These successes in defeating superior and better-equipped forces reinforce their belief that the West can, and should, be taken head on since it does not have the will to fight dedicated soldiers. Such Muslims believe that they can become a force to be reckoned with and, consequently, be respected by the West.

Financial crises

Saudi Arabia

Oil-rich Saudi Arabia was one of the wealthiest countries in the Middle East. However, after the Gulf War, its financial situation deteriorated considerably. For months, the government did not pay many local businesses and individuals. At one stage, the Saudi government sought help from international credit markets to help tide over its budget deficit. In 2001, the budget shortfall was $7 billion, more than 10 percent of revenues. The estimated 2002 shortfall is $12 billion. It has been estimated that the total Saudi debt by the end of 2002 will be $180 billion—a backbreaking burden.

News of the Saudi financial crisis shocked Muslims throughout the world. The deterioration in the financial health of Saudi Arabia, with billions of dollars in oil revenues, was totally unexpected. The common Muslim perception is that the Saudis were forced to bankroll the Desert

Storm operation, which drained them financially. Since then, the Saudi military budget has also gone up considerably due to weapons purchases. A common perception among Muslims, which cannot be verified, is that the Saudis are paying part of the cost of maintaining American troops in Saudi Arabia, which continues to drain them more than 10 years after the Gulf War.

Bank of Credit and Commerce

The Bank of Credit and Commerce (BCCI) was a well-run bank primarily owned by Muslims. During the Afghanistan-Soviet war, it played a major role in the transfer of weapons and funds across countries. BCCI was aggressive in its expansion plans and seemed to be on track to become a major international banking entity. However, it committed a serious mistake when it made a deal to finance the socialist government of Jamaica, which did not want to accept aid from an international lending agency because of unacceptable terms.

According to Muslims, the BCCI action raised a red flag in Western governments. They claim that the West did not want a Muslim bank to become powerful and have the financial strength to make such deals even though the amount of the Jamaican agreement was relatively small. The deal indicated that the bank could move on to bigger deals in more sensitive countries, which could impact the West's foreign policy and dilute its political clout. Therefore, the West declared BCCI bankrupt and seized its assets. According to Muslim bankers, the bank was solvent. This theory is plausible considering the fact that the BCCI shareholders and depositors received very high payouts after bankruptcy proceedings, which was much higher than in similar insolvencies.

Leadership losses

For the first time in the 20th century, the Muslim world started to think and act collectively in the political and economic arena when King Feisal of Saudi Arabia, a political and religious leader, and Zulfikar

Ali Bhutto of Pakistan, a charismatic leader and brilliant strategist, started to work together as a potent team.

Feisal was one of the most respected Muslim leaders in modern history. A religious man, he led a simple and austere life despite the wealth that flowed to the Saudi royal family. His principles, independent thinking, and leadership skills made him an admired man throughout the Muslim world. He was also one of the architects of the 1973 Arab oil embargo against the West. In 1975, a Saudi prince who had lived for a while in the United States murdered him. Feisal's murder sent a shock wave through the Muslim world. The common, although unproven, belief among Muslims is that the mentally unstable prince was used as a tool by the Americans to eliminate Feisal because he was an independent thinker and, consequently, posed a threat to their interests in the Middle East.

Bhutto was overthrown in 1977 in an army coup led by General Zia-ul-Haq. He was accused of being involved in a murder, found guilty by a corrupt justice system that usually followed political winds instead of truth, and hanged in 1979. The common perception among Muslims is that America wanted Bhutto eliminated for two reasons. First, he was the brains behind the united actions of the Muslims. Second, he was serious about making Pakistan a nuclear power. According to Pakistanis, Kissinger warned Bhutto that unless he rolled back his nuclear ambitions, America would make an example of him, which they did through their ally, the dictator Zia-ul-Haq.

Pakistan's nuclear bomb

Pakistan, a highly illiterate country, is one of the poorest nations in the world with an extremely backward technology infrastructure. When Bhutto took power in 1971, he embarked on a program to produce a nuclear bomb. His decision was based on the realization that Pakistan could never win a conventional war against India, which had just defeated Pakistan and caused its breakup. To neutralize militarily a country 10 times bigger, he needed a powerful deterrent. Since only a nuclear bomb could achieve that objective, he launched a nuclear program that was ultimately successful.

Muslims throughout the world are proud of the Pakistani achievement, made possible by a few engineers and scientists with access to limited resources. It confirms their belief that Muslims are second to none when they are dedicated and work with a purpose. The success of Pakistan's nuclear program is one of the few events in recent history that has elevated the morale of Muslims worldwide. It has given them confidence that they can emulate the performance of Muslims during the Golden Age of Islam.

CHAPTER 4

PERCEIVED WESTERN ROLE AND MUSLIM REACTION

ROLE PLAYED BY AMERICA AND WESTERN POWERS

Support for Israel

According to widespread belief among Muslims, American policy has always been one-sided in the Arab-Israeli conflict, with the exception of its stand in the 1956 Suez Canal crisis. As Muslims are quick to point out, America has barely murmured at the following Israeli actions many of which have been documented in reports published by international human rights organizations:

- ❑ Denial of due process to the occupied population of Palestine
- ❑ Arbitrary and punitive blowing up of homes; destruction of orchards and agricultural and industrial installations, as reported by Amnesty International
- ❑ Daily atrocities and humiliations carried out against the Palestinians

- Acting as an occupation power for 35 years
- Illegal occupation of Arab lands
- Expansion of settlements
- Targeted assassinations
- Massacre of two thousand Palestinian civilians at the Sabra and Shatila camps by the Lebanese Phalange Christian militia, who were permitted by the Israeli army to enter the camps (that were under Israeli control)
- Violation of American law (when Israeli forces use American-supplied weapons against civilians)
- Violation of the Fourth Geneva Convention, which includes prohibitions against willful killings and extensive destruction and appropriation of property not justified by military necessity
- Refusal to implement UN resolutions including Resolution 242, which mandated withdrawal of Israeli forces from Palestinian territories occupied in the 1967 war
- Abuse of human rights including torture and ill treatment during interrogation; Amnesty International has reported that there is credible evidence of serious violations of international humanitarian law and human rights by Israeli forces in Jenin (Palestine)

According to Muslims, even two or three of the above actions would have drawn America's wrath if the perpetrator had been any country other than Israel. Since American aid and armaments have provided the fuel in the Israeli engine, it is not surprising that the Palestinians and large segments of the Arab and Muslim populations hate Americans.

According to one segment of Muslims, the Israeli action in dispossessing the Palestinians is remarkably similar to what the Americans did to Native Americans. Hence, their belief is that Americans either see no wrong in what the Israelis have done to the Palestinians, as it is similar to what they themselves have done, or they cannot preach to the Israelis because their own history is not spotless.

Soft attitude towards Israeli leadership

At the height of the Israeli invasion of the West Bank in April 2002, when Palestinian towns were being invaded and destroyed, President Bush praised Israeli Prime Minister Ariel Sharon as a "Man of Peace." There is a serious disconnect between the perceptions of Mr. Bush and others who are familiar with the Middle East and Sharon. For example, in the *New York Times* of April 21, 2002, former President Jimmy Carter wrote the following about Sharon:

"His rejection of all peace agreements that included withdrawal from Arab land, his invasion of Lebanon, his provocative visit to the Temple Mount, the destruction of villages and homes, the arrests of thousands of Palestinians and his open defiance of President George W. Bush's demand that he comply with international law have all been orchestrated to accomplish his ultimate goals: to establish Israeli settlements as widely as possible throughout occupied territories and to deny Palestinians a cohesive political existence."

Since July 2001, Sharon has been under investigation by a Belgium magistrate for alleged crimes against humanity for his role in the Sabra and Shatila massacres. He was the Israeli defense minister in 1982 when Palestinian men, women, and children were systematically killed by the Lebanese Phalangist Christian militia, the allies of the Israelis, in cold blood at the Sabra and Shatila refugee camps in Lebanon over a three-day period. While Israeli forces sealed the camps and provided protection, the Phalangists militiamen went on a rampage, killing civilians and mutilating their bodies. According to most estimates, the number of people butchered is about two thousand, though Israeli estimates put the number at eight hundred.

Human Rights Watch has taken the position that the killings at the Sabra and Shatila camps constitute war crimes and crimes against humanity. The Kahan Israeli Commission of Inquiry, in its report on the massacres, found Sharon guilty of indirect responsibility for the slaughter. Sharon was found responsible for ignoring the danger of bloodshed and revenge when he approved the entry of the Phalangist militia into the camps as well as not taking appropriate measures to prevent bloodshed. Others who were held responsible included Prime Minister Menachem Begin, Foreign Minister Yitzhak Shamir, and Chief of Staff Rafael Eitan. Despite negative findings against them, they continued to rise politically and two, Shamir and Sharon, rose to the prime minister's post.

It is obvious that there is a tremendous disconnect when the same person is viewed so differently by several groups. Not surprisingly, America is hated because it is perceived to provide special treatment to the Israelis and consistently ignore atrocities against Palestinians and, hence, Muslims.

Support for despots and dictators

There are very few democratic Muslim countries at this time. Unelected rulers, including a large number of despots and dictators, rule most of them. Many current leaders came to power through democratic means but became dictators after consolidating power. While some suppress only those who oppose them, others maintain power by ruthlessly suppressing everyone. A common grievance of Muslims in many oppressed countries is that their rulers are, or were, being actively supported or aided by America and other Western powers. For example, at some time or other, America supported Saddam Hussein, Zia-ul-Haq, Sukarno, and the Shah of Iran, all of whom violated human rights for more than a decade in each case.

Judging by, and imposing, foreign values

Muslims complain that, by and large, the Western world has a one-sided view of what occurs in Muslim countries and societies. They feel that the West does not realize that the value systems of other countries, especially Muslim, are different from its own. It does not appreciate the fact that differences in values extend to personal, family, social, economic, legal, religious, and government areas. According to Muslims, the West is decadent in moral values because it permits abortion, supports gay rights, is lenient towards criminals, etc. Therefore, it cannot take a high moral ground or judge Muslims. According to those supporting this argument, since America does not allow others to impose their values on it, it should not impose its values on Muslims.

Insensitivity to Muslim feelings

Following the Gulf War, Americans were allowed by the Saudi government to establish military bases in Saudi Arabia. That decision has caused considerable resentment among a large segment of the Saudi population, who consider the presence of American troops a sacrilege. Many Muslims throughout the world also view the presence of non-Muslim soldiers in Saudi Arabia quite negatively.

Hatred for the American way of life

A large number of American politicians and the overwhelming majority in the media, especially talk show hosts, have incorrectly attributed Muslim antagonism towards America to their hatred for the "American and Western way of life" and its democratic traditions. According to those who subscribe to this theory, Muslims hate American values, its prosperity, and everything else it stands for. Therefore, because they are jealous, they want to destroy Western civilization and everything associated with it.

Media bias

According to Muslims, the American media tends to present a one-sided view of Arabs, Muslims, and issues associated with them. They point out that the bias is broad-based and includes newspapers, magazines, books, TV, and radio. The worst offenders are the live radio talk show hosts who, with their large audiences and lack of editorial fetters, perpetuate or reinforce negative perceptions about Muslims. A large number regularly spew hatred against Muslims and one has even called for a Holocaust against Palestinians. They often take an unrepresentative or odd act with which a Muslim individual or country is associated and use it to denigrate all Muslims by creating the perception that such actions are the norm. What upsets Muslims tremendously is that much of what is said on the air by biased talk show hosts is pure fiction.

Many knowledgeable Americans are also upset at what is aired by such hosts because of stereotyping, and the mixing of opinions with facts, which has been known to hurt Muslims as well as other groups in American society including Jews and gays. The nature of the shows is such that it is next to impossible for station management to micromanage how and what is being said on the air waves.

Friendship of convenience

Pakistan joined the American-led CENTO and SEATO defense pacts in the 1950s. For years, Pakistan was considered a dependable and trusted friend by America, which used it for its secret U-2 spy flights over the Soviet Union. However, Pakistan's interests took a back seat in 1962 when its arch-enemy India was defeated by the Chinese in a localized war. To the Americans, India became more valuable as a potential ally against Communist China because it was larger and more strategic than Pakistan.

In the 1980s, Pakistan suddenly became important again to America because it could be used as a tool in the proxy war against the Soviets in Afghanistan. Therefore, America poured military and economic aid into Pakistan. However, as soon as the Soviet army lost the war and retreated, Pakistan again fell out of favor. Old issues that had been conveniently ignored (including nuclear development, terrorism, and human rights) suddenly became important again and Pakistan came very close to being declared a terrorist state. After 9-11, Pakistan once again became valuable because of its potential to help in the war on terrorism and bring the perpetrators of 9-11 to justice.

In the friendship-of-convenience context, Afghanistan is another example cited by Muslims. It was used by America as a tool to fight the Soviet Union. When the Soviets were defeated, the Americans walked away, leaving behind a shattered country in dire need of political stability and economic aid.

The widespread perception among Muslims is that the Americans are only interested in friendships of convenience. The only exception, as they perceive it, is America's support of Israel, which they view as an anti-Muslim country. Another widespread belief is that the "friendship" with Arab oil countries will end the day America's need for Middle East oil goes away.

Double standards

Muslims believe that America does not use the same criteria for Muslims that it uses for itself or its friends. Muslims believe that when it stands to benefit, America either ignores or actively supports violations of its own principles. In a large number of such cases, the sufferers have been Muslims. For example, the Algerian Islamic Salvation Front swept the first-round of national elections in 1991. However, the army intervened and stopped the election process because it did not want the Salvation Front to take power. The army action triggered a bloody civil war that is still continuing. Muslims believe Americans and the West chose to ignore the hijacking of the election results and the Algerian army's brutal repression of its own people because the Islamic Front, with its independent ideology, did not fit into their strategic plans.

When Saddam Hussein was America's friend and actively supported by it in the 1980s, he used chemical weapons to attack his Kurd opponents. More than five thousand people were gassed to death in a single town, Halabja, in 1988. The Americans did not take any meaningful action against Saddam, even though they were horrified and troubled by future implications of the event, because he served their strategic interest of containing Iran.

In 1990, when America needed to build a coalition for the Gulf War, it enlisted the support of Hafez al-Assad, the same tyrant who sent his murderous troops into the Syrian town of Hama on February 2, 1982. During a four-week period, Assad's forces massacred more than ten thousand civilians. Many estimates of the number killed are as high as thirty-eight thousand.

America has used UN resolutions to justify its military and economic actions against Iraq. However, it has chosen to be selective in deciding which resolutions should be implemented. For example, America has ignored Israel's refusal since 1967 to implement UN resolution 242 mandating its withdrawal from occupied Palestinian territories. It has also ignored India's refusal to implement UN resolutions, passed in the 1950s, that promised Kashmiris the right of self-determination. America has also ignored India's gross human rights violations in Kashmir because there has been no compelling self-interest. It also ignored fundamental and human rights abuses committed during the 11-year dictatorship of General Zia-ul-Haq, who broke his promise to hold elections within 90 days of overthrowing Bhutto, because he served American interests in Afghanistan.

Post-Gulf War Iraq policy

The common Muslim view is that the Americans left Saddam Hussein in power after the Gulf War, even though they disliked him and could easily have removed him, because they wanted him to serve their strategic interests in the Middle East. Since his departure would have made Iran very powerful and dangerous, America decided to let Saddam stay in power so that he could be used as a counterweight to the anti-American Iranians. However, since the Americans did not want an unfettered and adventurous Saddam on the loose, they decided to clip his wings with the expectation that he could be quickly rearmed and used, if required. Therefore, after the war ended in 1991, an economic embargo was imposed on Iraq that is still in effect. The embargo has caused severe hardship and deprivation for ordinary Iraqis. While the ruling class continues to live comfortably, life for most citizens is an endurance test that never seems to end.

Children suffer the most from the embargo. It has been estimated that more than half a million Iraqi children have died from malnutrition or lack of health care. When history books are finally written, this may be considered one of the worst tragedies in human history because it was preventable. For now, it is one of the primary factors causing Muslims throughout the world to view America and the West negatively. Even Muslims who have no sympathy for Saddam Hussein are appalled at the suffering endured by innocent people and, therefore, view the West and America very negatively on this issue.

Not differentiating between terrorism and freedom struggles

Injustice and oppression are widespread in the world today and have bred many trouble spots. In recent years, seething troubles have escalated into armed revolts. However, even though many uprisings are genuine and deserve to be classified as wars of liberation, they have been slapped with the terrorist label by America. The reason for such classification, typically, has been due to the terrorist acts committed by some members of the liberation movements or associated fringe groups.

In Kashmir, which historically was one of the most peaceful places in the world, more than seven hundred thousand Indian troops have been unsuccessfully trying since 1989 to suppress a small population of seven million. Indian occupation forces kill an average of 20 civilians every day, and this has gone on for years. If such behavior is not state-terrorism, Muslims ask, then what is? Also, despite having one of the worst records of human rights abuses in the 20th century, India has not been condemned by Americans. Instead, they have restricted their criticism to a few fringe Kashmiri groups whose members have committed terrorist acts.

The issue that Muslims have is that the West, and particularly America, has not criticized friendly nations committing state-sponsored terrorism with the same level of outrage as it has exhibited for others. For example both India and Israel have been perpetuating state-sponsored terrorism for decades against, respectively, the Kashmiris and Palestinians. While they have been right in criticizing criminal terrorist acts by some Kashmiri groups, Hamas, Islamic Jehad, and other PLO groups, they should have exerted their influence to rein in the Indians and the Israelis. The Indians routinely torture suspects, rape women, and burn down shops, homes, and villages in reprisals as has been documented by many international human rights organizations. The Israelis routinely blow up Palestinian homes without due process, perform targeted assassinations, and have been in violation of international law for the treatment of civilians in occupied territories, and its leaders are under investigation in Belgium for alleged crimes against humanity. While it is acknowledged that the terrorism perpetuated against Israeli civilians is un-Islamic and criminal, it does not justify illegal and morally unacceptable Israeli actions which, when carried out by a state, can be categorized as state-sponsored terrorism.

Divide and rule

As is widely taught in many schools in their former colonies, the British were the masters of the divide-and-rule policy that enabled them to be successful colonists. This policy was widely used in both Muslim and non-Muslim countries. However, the Muslim perception is that the destructive policy was primarily applied against them. It either resulted in Muslim countries fighting among themselves (or with their neighbors) or laid the seeds for future conflict among nations or ethnic groups, including conflicts such as Arabs versus Turks, Iraq versus Kuwait, Pakistan versus India, and Arabs versus Israelis.

According to Muslims, the incentive for the divide-and-rule policy was to weaken target countries economically and to ensure a good market for British armaments. Muslims feel that their countries have been sucked into a trap that has caused billions of dollars to be spent on defense instead of productive investments. Unfortunately, even though they want to, such countries cannot find a way out due to the legacy of hate as well as a lack of innovative and sincere leadership.

Islamic bomb

In 1974, India detonated a nuclear device and called it a "peaceful nuclear explosion." It did not elicit any noteworthy negative reaction from Western powers. They accepted, at face value, India's claim that it was a "peaceful" explosion even though there can be no real differentiation between a "peaceful" and an "aggressive" explosion (or bomb). Both types of explosions use the same basic principles and technology and both are capable of producing death and destruction.

Similarly, Israel has been producing nuclear weapons for a long time. Since it was an American ally, the U.S. chose to ignore its nuclear program. That attitude was in stark contrast to its view of the Pakistani nuclear program, which it tried to stop. Western media have been calling the Pakistani weapon the "Islamic bomb," even though the Israeli and Indian bombs were never called the Jewish or Hindu bombs. To Muslims, this is another item in a long list that reflects the bias of those who desire to create anti-Islam hysteria.

REACTION BY MUSLIMS TO RECENT HISTORICAL EVENTS

Refusing to accept responsibility

A defining characteristic of Muslims is to avoid acknowledging their own responsibility. They tend to blame others for their problems and poor condition. This attitude encompasses political, economic, social, and personal aspects of life.

If a country's leader defers to the Americans, Muslims blame America instead of blaming themselves for electing that leader or creating conditions that led him to make a compromise. If corruption inside their country is rampant, they will blame modernization and the influence of the West instead of blaming themselves for becoming dishonest at the personal level. According to Islam, the person who offers a bribe is as guilty as the person who accepts it. Applying that principle, the responsibility for corruption within each Muslim country lies with its own citizens. Muslims should be careful in analyzing the root cause of a problem and, when applicable, accept their own responsibility instead of finding excuses.

Advocating return to the seventh century

A small minority of Muslims do accept responsibility for the state of affairs that exists in Islamic countries and societies. They believe that the deterioration in the condition of Muslims and their countries is due to deviation from the teachings of Islam and decline in personal attributes and characteristics. There are two subgroups that acknowledge their mistakes. The first group stresses that Muslims should become modernized, continue to use Islamic principles, and make a determined effort to progress in the secular world. The second group is mainly composed of diehard fundamentalists, who advocate the implementation of a system that, while removing those things they see as vices, will economically take the Muslims back almost 14 centuries.

Feeling victimized

A fairly common feeling among Muslims is that the West and America are victimizing them. The daily barrage of negative news emanating from many Muslim countries, as well as from countries with Muslim minorities, continues to reinforce that belief. Many Muslims believe that the Western world is after them and cannot tolerate their economic uplift or political independence.

A widespread perception is that Europeans never really ended the Crusades or their colonial occupation because they still call the shots, though remotely. Many Muslims have become paranoid and tend to weave every issue and problem facing Muslims into a conspiracy by the West. For example, some Muslims have subscribed to the ludicrous view that 9-11 was an American plot whose ultimate aim was to occupy Afghanistan in order to control access to Central Asian oil.

Passive hatred

In many parts of the world, especially in the Middle East where the Palestinian issue is highly emotional and America is perceived as the power behind the Israeli oppressor's guns, a large percentage of Muslims hate America. However, such hatred is not deep, except in Middle East core flashpoints, and is primarily directed at American policies and government, not its citizens. The hatred is not caused by jealousy, the American way of life, or its prosperity as some Americans have incorrectly tried to portray. Instead, it can be attributed to the unquestioning support America has provided to Israel, which has suppressed the Palestinians and occupied their lands since 1967. Knowledgeable Muslims reiterate with confidence that when America starts to act impartially in the Middle East, as it did in 1956, the Muslims' hate for it will dissipate.

Among the Muslims who hate America are two distinct groups. The first group consists of people who hate America passively. The overwhelming majority of those who hate America belong to this group. The second group is consumed by hatred that they want to translate into action. These Muslims are primarily drawn from the central area of suffering—Palestine and the Middle East. However, Muslims with such feelings can be found in practically every Muslim country, though their numbers are not large or significant except in the Middle East and Iran.

Acting prejudiced

There is a small minority of Muslims so prejudiced against the West and America that they will never change their views, no matter what happens or which facts are brought to their attention. They will ignore or dismiss any fair and even-handed actions by the West or Jews. For example, these people ignore or dismiss the fact that the most vocal critics of the West's policies in Bosnia, when Muslims were being butchered, were Jews. The Jewish community was in the forefront in the attempt to publicize the ethnic cleansing of Bosnian Muslims by the Serbs.

The Muslims in the prejudiced category have also dismissed the fact that the West helped end the Kosovo war by undertaking a massive bombing campaign against Serbia in 1999. They have also not given credit to the West for ultimately bringing Milosovich, the Serbian strongman, to justice.

Most members belonging to this minority group of Muslims are passive. Their activities are limited to discussing, arguing, and complaining.

Becoming freedom fighters or terrorists

In various countries or regions that have become occupied or oppressed in recent times, many Muslims have taken the path of armed resistance. The recruits for armed struggles in such places, typically, are not deeply religious or practicing Muslims. Many became freedom fighters or terrorists only when their country or region was oppressed and justice and freedom were denied. They chose the path of armed resistance because of their circumstances.

There are many Muslim freedom fighters who fight with groups having an Islamic name. In many cases, the Islamic label can be quite misleading because the fighters, in reality, are nationalists. They do not follow any particular ideology, are not deeply religious and, in some cases, are not even practicing Muslims. The majority of fighters in Kashmir, Palestine, and Chechnya fall in the nationalist movement category.

Exporting mujahideen and terrorists

In the recent past, the freedom struggles of Muslims in countries such as Afghanistan and Bosnia have attracted fighters from other countries. Typically, radical fundamentalists driven by religious zeal answered the call for jehad in Afghanistan. Most of them lacked knowledge about the world, history, and current events. Even their knowledge about Islam was limited to basic rituals and elementary Islamic history. In most cases, they did not understand the background or the cause of the conflict in the foreign country that they went to fight. All that they knew was that a jehad was in progress and that mujahideen were needed to help Muslims who were being suppressed or killed. It was easy for scheming leaders to use such people as foot soldiers for a wrong cause. The Taliban and al-Qaeda demonstrated this in Afghanistan, where low-level recruits were enlisted.

Another extremely small but very motivated group of Muslims prefers to use a different method of attack. Instead of fighting on battlegrounds, they become urban terrorists who focus on bombing civilian and commercial targets. While some have acted alone or in small groups, a few have been guided and used by countries that sponsor state-terrorism.

These two radical groups are the ones Muslims need to fear. They have the potential to harm the genuine causes and aspirations of ordinary Muslims. The first group can be misused and misguided into joining questionable causes. The second group's activities are counter to Islamic principles and cannot be tolerated or condoned by civilized people.

9-11: THE HIJACKING OF ISLAM

Why it happened

September 11, 2001, is a day of infamy when the terrorist group al-Qaeda, led by Osama bin Laden, hijacked Islam. On that day a devastating, concerted terrorist attack was launched on America in the name of Islam. Suicide pilots flew hijacked commercial aircraft into the World Trade Center in New York City and the Pentagon. The attack resulted in the collapse of the World Trade Center Twin Towers and the death of thousands of innocent civilians, including more than two hundred Muslims.

The successful terrorist attacks, driven by hatred for the United States, were the latest attempt by the al-Qaeda organization to hit American targets. It had previously engaged in terrorist attacks against American interests in many parts of the world. The motivation for the attacks was bin Laden's bitter resentment of the presence of American troops in Saudi Arabia as well as American foreign policy, which he viewed as anti-Islamic.

Osama bin Laden, a Saudi Arabian exile, planned the 9-11 attacks from his base in Afghanistan, where he operated under the patronage of the ruling Taliban government. He had previously fought against the Soviet army during the Afghanistan war in the 1980s. After the war ended, he expanded al-Qaeda into a worldwide terrorist organization. He funded the organization using his huge inheritance that, by some accounts, had grown to more than $300 million. The organization he built attracted thousands of recruits, brimming with religious zeal and resentment, from all over the Muslim world.

Anti-Islamic act

The terrorists who participated in the 9-11 attack violated many fundamental Islamic principles. First, they killed innocent civilians, which is expressly prohibited by Islam. According to Islam, as is clearly stated in the Koran, the taking of an innocent life is equivalent to the killing of all mankind. In this case, the hijackers killed thousands of innocent people. Second, they committed suicide, which is an unforgivable sin in Islam. Third, they killed more than two hundred Muslims who were working in the World Trade Center. Fourth, one of the hijackers was reported to have been drinking alcohol in Florida the night before the attacks. No Muslim who truly respects Islam and its principles will ever drink alcohol, especially just before certain death, since it is strictly prohibited in Islam. The simple fact is that an evil man used the name of Islam and violated Islamic principles in order to achieve his reprehensible and murderous objectives.

How Muslims view the 9-11 tragedy

American Muslims were shocked, with an initial sense of disbelief, when the perpetrators of the 9-11 crime were identified. An overwhelming majority of Muslims view the event as a heinous crime and are engulfed by a profound sense of sorrow. They cannot comprehend how innocent civilians could be targeted in the name of Islam. Subsequently, personal safety and the effect on day-to-day lives by the sudden spurt in hate crimes resulting from the tragedy became a common concern of most American Muslims. Other concerns regarding how the event and its fallout will impact everyone are similar to those felt by other ordinary Americans.

Throughout the world also, Muslims have classified 9-11 as a crime when provided with details of the attack and its destruction. That has been especially true when they received their news through television rather than through sources that did not provide graphic details. The exception to this view is in the Middle East, where America is considered synonymous with Israel and oppression and, hence, is hated.

There is a very small minority of Muslims who do not view the 9-11 event as an unprovoked crime. They rationalize the actions of bin Laden from a global perspective, viewing America as the unjust supporter of oppressors and tyrants. A few believe in the ridiculous theory that the terrorist attack was part of an American plot whose objective was to occupy Afghanistan.

Even though an overwhelming majority of Muslims consider the 9-11 terrorist attack wrong and against Islamic principles, some also tend to view it from an Islamic religious perspective. They view it as the punishment and retribution for a wrongdoer. According to Islam, God has His own ways of equalizing or punishing injustice that sometimes occurs through unexpected ways to hurt or destroy an evil power, ruler, or individual. Hence, they view this tragedy as God's way of bringing home to America what it had exported to the Palestinians and others in many parts of the world.

Impact on Muslims

The 9-11 terrorist attack has been a defining event and wake-up call for Muslims, especially in America. It has finally forced mainstream Muslims to realize that unless they act and take control, they will have to dance to the tune of the more radical elements that use Islam as a tool for implementing an agenda that is unacceptable to the overwhelming majority of Muslims. 9-11 and the Osama-induced polarization within the community has caused Muslims, especially leaders, to perform serious self-analysis. It has led mainstream Muslims and moderate leaders to become more vocal and involved in community discussions where, typically, radical fundamentalist elements once took the leadership role by default due to their "religious" and "righteous" bent.

CHAPTER 5

WHERE LIES THE TRUTH

Many issues have caused problems between Muslims and the Western world, especially America. Each group faults the other and, in most cases, they view the same event from completely different perspectives. Not surprisingly, they reach diametrically opposite conclusions. If their complaints and perceptions are analyzed closely and impartially, it becomes obvious that there are faults in perception as well as action on both sides.

The previous two chapters identified and described many defining events and crises that have shaped Muslim thinking and attitudes vis-à-vis the West. Additionally, the Muslim viewpoint regarding those events and crises was presented. This chapter presents an analysis of the major issues that have soured relations and produced distrust between Muslims and the West and, additionally, caused America to be hated by Muslims worldwide.

The truth lies somewhere between what is perceived by the Muslims and by the West. The objective of Muslim-American relations should be to have a better understanding of the issues rather than to find fault so that bridges can be built between the two sides. Unless both sides are prepared to identify and acknowledge their mistakes and failings, lasting solutions cannot be found and a better future cannot be hoped for.

ANALYZING MUSLIM COMPLAINTS AGAINST AMERICA

American support for Israel is one-sided

The history of American support for Jews goes back to 1946, even before the creation of Israel. According to *Time* magazine, in its 1951 "Man of the Year" issue, "To catch the Jewish vote in the U.S., President Truman in 1946 demanded that the British admit one hundred thousand Jewish refugees to Palestine, in violation of British promises to the Arabs. Since then, the Arab nations surrounding Israel have regarded the state as a U.S. creation, and the U.S., therefore, as an enemy. The Israeli-Arab war created nearly a million Arab refugees, who have been huddled for three years in wretched camps. These refugees, for whom neither the U.S. nor Israel will take the slightest responsibility, keep alive the hatred of U.S. perfidy."

American public opinion has been solidly in favor of Israel over the years. Support has remained steady despite the Israeli occupation of Palestine and its oppressive actions as an occupation force for more than 35 years. Americans have tended to ignore Israeli atrocities as well as their violation of human rights and the Geneva Convention. Occupation forces are required to follow international rules and laws in their treatment of civilians in occupied areas, but Israel has violated them repeatedly, knowing that America will protect it.

Americans are among the most fair-minded people in the world, yet they have turned a blind eye to Israeli atrocities and oppression, demonized the Arabs and Palestinians, and blamed them for virtually every crisis. The dichotomy regarding the Israeli-Palestinian problem, and the one-sided American view, can be attributed to lack of information and knowledge. The vast majority of Americans have been either uninformed or misinformed about the Middle East crisis. Prior to 9-11, most of them had, at best, a vague idea of its history, developments, and current status—which has no similarity with the 1948 situation when Israel was a young nation with hostile neighbors. At that time, the unconditional support of the West could be understood and respected by moderate Muslims.

However, despite Israel's transition from a country in danger to an expansionist power, America has been unwavering in its support for Israel. For Americans, it is simply a case of good versus bad, and the Palestinians have always been bad while the Israelis have always been victims. Since the Arab oil embargo of 1973, Americans have crystallized their negative opinion of Arabs and Palestinians on the basis of one-sided news that tended to stereotype Arabs and blame them, and OPEC, for the lifestyle disruptions and higher costs for gasoline, home heating, etc. Also contributing to the negative view were some high-profile terrorist acts perpetuated by the Palestinians starting with the killing of Israeli Olympic athletes. However, Israeli actions over the years, many of which have been illegal and systematic, have not been taken as seriously as the Palestinian transgressions and, consequently, have not had any measurable impact on American public opinion polls.

It should be pointed out that there does exist a very small minority of Americans who are very well informed. However, their influence on public opinion is insignificant due to their small number.

Jewish influence in the Senate is too strong

The Muslim perception of American Middle East foreign policy being heavily influenced by Israel and American Jews does have some basis. An analysis of representation in Congress reveals disproportionate Jewish representation in the Senate. In early 2002, there are:
- 13 Catholic senators while Catholics account for 22 percent of the U.S. population
- 10 Jewish senators while Jews account for only 2 percent of the U.S. population

Those who understand demographics and how they impact elections in any country realize that a community or group with only two percent of the population would be considered lucky if it managed to achieve even one percent representation at the national, or Senate, level. While Muslims in America have a population almost equal to that of Jews, they have no representation in either the Senate or the House of Representatives.

Muslims believe that since 10 percent of the Senate is Jewish, Israel is practically immune from adverse American pressure. They complain that Israel knows that as well and, hence, acts accordingly. A perusal of the Senate record shows that one-sided and broad-based support for Israel is not limited to Jewish senators. Some of the most anti-Palestinian senators are not Jews. Also, it seems unlikely that 10 Jewish senators can consistently direct or influence 90 non-Jewish senators.

A probable explanation for the pro-Jewish sentiment in Congress is that Americans have been exposed to consistently negative reporting about Arabs and Palestinians since 1973—when the Arab oil embargo caused severe dislocation in the lifestyle of Americans, high energy bills, and long gas lines. For decades the thinking of ordinary Americans has been molded and reinforced by negative stereotyped images to a point where Americans believe Israelis are virtuous and Palestinians evil, even though that does not reflect reality. It should be realized that senators, representatives of an American population that views Arabs and Palestinians negatively, are highly unlikely to vote against their constituents' wishes. Unless the American population changes its views, Palestinians cannot expect most senators to change their current leanings.

Palestine issue incorrectly projected as religious struggle

Israel and the American media, as well as Muslim leaders and media, have projected the Palestinian struggle as a religious movement. However, the fact is that the Palestinian struggle has been a national liberation movement against Israeli occupation in which both Muslim and Christian Palestinians have participated with equal fervor. Secular-minded leaders who did not have any religious agenda initially led the movement. The most popular leader was Yasser Arafat and the main opposition group was the Palestine Liberation Organization (PLO), an umbrella group of twenty organizations that included leftists and rightists.

In order to weaken the secular PLO by making religious organizations strong, Israel encouraged and nurtured organizations such as Hamas. For a while, Hamas confined itself to social work and became very popular. Over time, it became a political force and, not surprisingly, started armed resistance against the Israelis. Hamas and other religious organizations became even more popular as Arafat's popularity declined and Palestinians lost faith in his ability to deliver freedom and control corruption in the Palestinian Authority. At this time, armed resistance against Israelis is spearheaded by Islamic religious groups, though it was not so during earlier stages of the struggle, and they are fully supported by both secular and Christian Palestinians.

The fault for the animosity, therefore, can be laid on both sides. The Muslims and Israelis, for their own ends, have been incorrectly projecting a national liberation struggle as a religious war. Additionally, the Muslims' lack of strong condemnation of suicide bombings, that are completely un-Islamic, has resulted in a genuine struggle being battered in the Western media. The Western press can be faulted because it has been focusing too much on recent events, without giving as much attention as it should to the root cause of the problem—the occupation of Palestine for 35 years.

America is anti-Islam and anti-Muslim

A widely held view among Muslims is that America is anti-Islam and anti-Muslim, which is not true. Contrary to this perception, the allegedly deleterious actions by America against Muslims cannot be attributed to an anti-Islam or religion-biased policy. Rather, they are the result of policies dictated by American security considerations, self-interest, and its economic dependence on a vital commodity—oil. Without oil, the American economy will grind to a halt. Hence, making oil supplies safe and reliable is at the top of American policymakers' priorities.

For America, security considerations, economic self-interest (including business interests of corporate America and military sales), and oil are the primary foreign policy drivers while other factors, also considered important, are sometimes forced to take a back seat due to conflicting priorities. There can be no denying American commitment to democracy and human rights. However, at times, they have been ignored due to the focus on issues that were perceived, sometimes incorrectly, to be more important due to three factors:

- Cold War and desire to contain communism
- Never-ending quest to ensure a cheap, safe, and steady supply of Middle East oil
- American hesitancy since the end of the Vietnam War to become militarily involved without clear objectives and an exit strategy

At no stage have American policies been dictated by the desire or plan to harm Muslim interests. In recent times, the interests of America and the Islamic world have not matched, hence the current conflict between the two. However, when it has suited America's interests it has befriended and helped Muslim countries. For example, it currently views Pakistan as a friend because of its help in the war on terrorism.

Support for despots and dictators

The Western powers have been very vocal in preaching democracy and human rights to the rest of the world. However, in violation of its own principles, America has supported some of the world's worst despots and human rights violators, in some cases for many years. American support over the years has included active involvement (such as overthrowing Mossadegh and reinstating the Shah), passive acquiescence, and massive economic and military aid.

Many of the worst dictators, despots, and corrupt leaders supported by the West have reigned in the Muslim world. They include:

- Saddam Hussein of Iraq
- Shah of Iran
- Hosni Mubarak of Egypt
- Zia-ul-Haq of Pakistan
- Sukarno of Indonesia
- Suharto of Indonesia
- Hafez al-Assad of Syria (though not supported, was a U.S. ally in the Gulf War)

In the countries where these leaders reigned, millions of people were suppressed, tortured, and brutalized for decades in the second half of the 20th century. For them, American calls for democracy and respect for human rights seem hollow and hypocritical.

An argument put forth in America's defense is that it supported many of the dictators at the height of the Cold War when security concerns were of paramount concern to American policy makers. The dictators were viewed as the lesser of two evils, compared to communism, who could be depended upon to provide stable governments, which were often lacking in Third World countries, and support the effort against communism.

Judging by, and imposing, foreign values

The typical American's knowledge about Islamic and Middle Eastern history, culture, and values is limited. This shortcoming is one of the primary reasons that Americans, unknowingly, take actions that are deemed insensitive by Muslims. Americans tend to make quick judgments regarding foreign issues and cultures based on superficial knowledge and without in-depth study. For example, the Afghan women's burqa, which is not mandated by Islam, has been overblown as an issue. It has been hyped to a point where Americans now consider its disappearance from Afghan society as a major goal that will liberate its women.

Americans do not realize that the Afghans, especially at this time, do not view the burqa as an important issue, if they consider it to be one at all. First, they have more pressing needs and issues such as safety and security, food, medical treatment, shelter, education, etc. Second, their women will continue using the burqa, which was introduced centuries ago, of their own free will because it is the norm in their society. It will take generations before Afghan women discard it, if at all, on their own initiative—not because Americans think it is a sign of oppression.

When Americans try to impose or suggest their own solutions to Muslim countries, even though they may do so with the best of intentions, the intrusion creates more harm than good. Compared to Americans, who are viewed as arrogant, Europeans are viewed as more considerate of differences with Muslims because they have had more interaction with Asian and African countries.

It is also pertinent to point out that this issue is not one-sided. Muslims too, are often prone to judge Americans based on superficial knowledge and without first ascertaining the facts. For example, most of them are completely unaware of the fact that America has a very large number of religious people, with an estimated 40-50 percent of the population considering themselves born-again Christians. Neither are they aware of the objectives, and strength, of the Religious Right (Christian Coalition) movement with whom they share many common values—without realizing it. They are also not aware that, as in the Islamic community, many people in the West oppose practices such as abortion even if they carry government approval.

Insensitivity to Muslim feelings

Muslims who complain about the presence of American troops in Saudi Arabia, due to religious reasons, cannot support their claim of sacrilege. Their objections are based on emotions and not any Islamic teachings. According to Islam, Mecca is the only city non-Muslims are specifically prohibited from entering. Muslims also consider Medina a holy city, but it is not restricted. However, most Muslims regard all of Saudi Arabia as a holy land although there is no scriptural basis for that belief.

There is no Islamic restriction on the presence of non-Muslims in Saudi Arabia. In fact, there are hundreds of thousands of Asian non-Muslims, especially from India and Japan, working in Saudi Arabia. However, their presence is not considered sacrilegious even though most of them do not believe in monotheism and, hence, are the worst sinners according to Islam—something that cannot be said about American Christians and Jews who are among the "People of the Book." Those who oppose the presence of American troops also tend to conveniently ignore the fact that tens of thousands of American oil experts have worked in Saudi Arabia, since the discovery of oil in the 1930s, and their presence was never opposed or considered sacrilegious.

It appears that either the potential of hurting Muslim feelings was underestimated or the decision was forced on the Saudi and American governments by a pressing need for regional security following the Gulf War, which had caused panic and security concerns among the smaller Arab Gulf countries. The common belief among Muslims is that the Saudis made the military bases deal with the Americans to ensure that the royal family, whose support is decreasing in a country with 15-20 percent unemployment, would have strong American military support in case domestic unrest threatened its hold on power.

Hatred for the American way of life

A widespread belief in America is that Muslims hate the American and Western way of life, which is not correct. Those who propound this theory either speak from ignorance or have a vested interest in deflecting the focus from the most important root cause of the American-Muslim problem—the Palestinian-Israeli issue.

The overwhelming majority of Muslims do not hate Americans, their prosperity, or their way of life. For most, to have the American life would be a dream come true. Muslims throughout the world are aware of America's high standard of living, personal freedom, and fundamental rights. They would love to be a part of that lifestyle if they could. However, they do hate American foreign policy that, in their view, is unjust and biased against Muslims and Islam. It is true that Muslims see behaviors in the West that Islam does not support, such as alcohol consumption, but this disapproval is not strong enough to provoke the kinds of negative reactions that result from the Palestinian issue.

A small percentage of Americans realize that there is a different side to the Middle East story. For example, Pat Buchanan wrote in his column at townhall.com on April 8, 2002, "America is not hated in that part of the world where we were once respected because we are democratic, prosperous and free. We are hated because of a deepening perception that the United States cannot conduct a policy independent of Israel's. We are hated because we have provided Israel with the weapons it has used not only to defeat Arab armies, but to annex land and crush Palestinian hopes."

Muslims do not hate or hope to destroy non-Christian countries for ways of life that conflict with Islamic beliefs. Therefore, it does not seem logical that Muslims would hate or wish to destroy any Christian country. Muslims know that most people in the West and America are Christians. Therefore, it does not make sense that Muslims would hate the way of life of a civilization whose moral values are based on Christianity, a sister religion.

American media is biased

American media have played a significant role in stereotyping Muslims and Arabs. They are, to a large extent, responsible for creating the image that Muslims and terrorists are synonymous. Mainstream Muslims do not have access to powerful media and cannot refute the news or misinformation disseminated by the media or unrepresentative Muslim extremists. The result of misinformation and projection of stereotyped images is that the opinion of Americans about Arabs and Muslims has become negative and biased. Since politicians act in accordance with constituents' wishes, there is a bias in American foreign policy against Arabs and Muslims. The net result of such policies has been that Americans are perceived by Muslims to be unjust and biased.

To be fair, the fault is not one-sided. Since the Muslim majority is silent, they have let the extremists, who are an insignificant minority, become their spokesmen by default. The Western media just pick up on what the extremists say and do and, consequently, the overall image of Muslims suffers considerably. The Western media can be faulted because they have not reported with diligence the views of the majority. They tend to focus on and project news that is more sensational. For example, the recent images of demonstrators flashed from Pakistan have consistently shown angry Muslim men shouting extremist slogans against America. A closer look will reveal that most of the demonstrators, and almost all the haranguing leaders, sport beards. Even a cursory study will reveal that such demonstrators do not represent the Pakistani society at large, where the bearded population is less than 10 percent! Such images create the incorrect impression that there is widespread support for religious extremists, who organized the demonstrations, even though the reality is quite different.

It is true that the American media have been incorrectly projecting the Arab-Israeli struggle as a religious struggle between the Muslims and Israelis. However, both Muslims and Israelis must be faulted for that because they too have projected the struggle as a religious one to suit their own ends. Though the armed Palestinian struggle for independence is now being led by Islamic groups, the very significant contribution of secular and Christian Palestinian freedom fighters, even at this time, has not been acknowledged adequately by any side.

In stark contrast to issues concerning Muslims, the same media have refrained, with some exceptions, from calling the Irish civil war between the Catholics and Protestants a religious war. While Palestinian terrorists are called Islamic terrorists, whether or not they are Muslims, the Irish Republican Army (IRA) terrorists have never been called Catholic terrorists even though all of them are Catholics who fight the Protestants in the name of religion.

Since 9-11, Americans have been seeking news and information rather than just waiting for them to come via established media. They have started to inform themselves by seeking information about Muslims and Islam, using unconventional sources such as the Internet and books. They have discovered that there is another side, a better one, of Muslims and Islam that they had not been aware of and that they can relate to.

News is driven by business needs

On any given day, only a couple of news stories are covered for more than a couple of minutes by American television networks. All other stories are delivered in two-and three-minute segments. Consequently, the coverage given each item is insufficient for anyone really to understand the story and its background. Such a news system, which is primarily driven by advertising dollars and the number of viewers tuning in, benefits the corporation operating the television or radio station. It seems not to serve the national interest, especially in the long run, because the net result is that viewers remain superficially informed about international issues even though they may be viewing the news regularly.

It needs to be pointed out that for those who have an interest, there is plenty of information provided in America through a variety of media including cable networks, public TV and radio, national newspapers, books, and magazines as well as a host of Internet sites. Prior to 9-11, there was no overriding interest and, hence, many of these sources remained untapped or underutilized.

A widespread complaint by Arabs and Muslims is that the American media does not adequately cover their viewpoints. It is true that only a limited amount of international, including Arab and Muslim, news is aired in America. The reason is that to a large extent, news coverage is driven by business needs and requirements that do not favor the broadcast of foreign news. The media likes to present stories that generate widespread interest, which typically are local and domestic rather than international, and pull in advertising dollars. Since international news does not attract many viewers and consequently, advertisers, its broadcast is limited due to financial considerations. However, this issue is not a unique American phenomenon. Most media throughout the world have the same domestic news focus, especially those operated on a for-profit basis. The only exceptions are the state-run television stations and government-controlled newspapers which suffer from three problems: lack of editorial independence, poor quality, and delayed reporting. Hence, people living in foreign countries are also not too well informed about American life and domestic issues, even though they may be knowledgeable about America's impact on world issues due to its importance as the only superpower.

Mujahideen were used and abandoned

During the war against the Soviet occupation forces in Afghanistan, numerous calls were made to Muslims throughout the world to join the jehad. Thousands of Muslims heeded the call and joined the war as mujahideen fighters. After the war ended, many of these fighters, especially those from Egypt and other Middle Eastern countries, could not return to their home countries. The reason was that their governments did not want battle-hardened, radical warriors to return home because they had the potential to create domestic problems and unrest. Also, many of the mujahideen belonged to banned organizations. With the fear of being arrested on their return, many of them stayed in Afghanistan and subsequently joined al-Qaeda.

The Americans and the West did not think beyond the end of the war against communism in Afghanistan. In contrast to returning American GIs who, over the years, were provided incentives and help in transitioning into civilian life and becoming productive citizens upon leaving the military, the mujahideen were abandoned. That poor decision, which was not made with bad intentions, created bitterness and a vacuum into which others, like bin Laden and the Taliban, stepped in. An issue that should have been relatively small was magnified into a serious international problem with far-reaching consequences.

America has acknowledged its mistake in walking away from Afghanistan after the Soviets were defeated which, directly and indirectly, harmed both Afghanistan and America. At this time, it is assisting in the formation of a representative government and has promised to provide aid to help rebuild Afghanistan.

Friendship of convenience

This perception is borne out by the facts. However, it should be pointed out that most of the American actions that are resented in many parts of the world, and not just in Muslim countries, were motivated by strategic concerns and took place in the second half of the 20th century—at the height of the Cold War. They were made with the intention of containing the Soviets—not with the intention of harming Muslims. If it appeared that a dictator might help in containing the communists, he was supported as the lesser of two evils. Such unpopular leaders were supported in all parts of the world—from Vietnam to Chile.

America has acknowledged, though belatedly, its mistakes in supporting tyrants in Iraq and other countries—policies for which it has and continues to pay a high price, especially through loss of goodwill and alienation of strategic partners.

Policy implemented by inexperienced politicians

In American presidential election campaigns, domestic priorities and issues drive the election agenda. International affairs get a back seat and, unless there is a major war or a crisis in progress, get little attention. Knowledge and mastery of international affairs are hardly tested during an election campaign. Consequently, a candidate can win and become president despite having only superficial knowledge of international affairs and world history. This has happened quite a few times in modern American history.

A president may be brilliant in his handling of domestic affairs. However, if he is unfamiliar with the complicated issues and problems characterizing foreign countries, his rookie status in foreign affairs gets highlighted immediately when an international crisis erupts. Unfortunately, time is too short to learn on the job. By the time a president with limited knowledge of foreign issues really starts to understand what is going on and masters the art of handling intractable foreign issues, his term is near its end or the problem has deteriorated and/or gotten out of hand.

The problem of American foreign policy being shaped or implemented by politicians with inadequate knowledge of foreign affairs and history is fairly widespread in both the legislative and executive branches. Such shortcomings exist at all levels and not just at the presidential level. Many members of Congress, including those who are members of influential foreign affairs committees, as well as cabinet members and White House advisors, also leave much to be desired so far as international experience and knowledge is concerned. While these politicians are masters of domestic politics, their unfamiliarity with foreign issues and their historical background is pervasive. Consequently, serious foreign policy mistakes are made with results that are not apparent for years and, thus, leave America with hidden and lingering problems that need to be addressed later on when they have become more serious.

Uninformed Americans

Americans have a domestic-centric view. Therefore, prior to 9-11, most of them had not exhibited more than a casual or superficial interest in foreign affairs, especially pertaining to events in the Middle East and Muslim countries. That was in stark contrast with their interest in domestic news and scandals, especially concerning domestic politicians and personalities. Consequently, as it did not impact their daily lives in the past, most Americans did not actively seek information about current world events and issues, Muslims, and Islam.

For topics of interest to them, Americans actively seek and devour any information they can obtain. Therefore, when the perpetrators of 9-11 were identified as Muslims, there was a dramatic rise in their interest in Muslims and Islam. Since then, they have used every means available to gain knowledge and understand the background leading up to the 9-11 terrorist attack. For most, it has been a revealing exercise as they learned that the world is more complicated than they had thought and, also, that their prior knowledge about Muslims and Islam was either incomplete, one-sided or incorrect.

The information that the vast majority of Americans receive is, by and large, through television network news, which does not provide in-depth coverage with the exception of some special programs. However, such detailed coverage is typically provided during times of crises. Even though there are many newspapers that provide foreign news coverage, and some are outstanding, the interest of most Americans is typically confined to domestic news, art, entertainment, sports, etc. Their lack of knowledge in the area of foreign affairs also has deeper roots. In high schools, Middle Eastern and Asian history is taught superficially. Even where one or two courses are taught, they are insufficient unless the knowledge gained is reinforced outside the class. Hence, a typical American high school graduate lacks adequate knowledge about the Middle East and its dynamics.

Typically, ordinary Americans used to be surprised when they had a lengthy one-on-one discussion with a Muslim colleague about Islam, Muslims, and the Middle East. More often than not, they would shake their heads in disbelief when they heard the other side of the story, especially concerning the Middle East conflict. A common comment used to be, "I had no idea about that!" However, the situation has changed considerably now. The research conducted by Americans after 9-11 as well as positive and constructive comments from leaders like President Bush, who need to be highly commended, have made a big difference in making them more informed and also improved their perception of Islam. This has been confirmed by public opinion polls, which indicate that since 9-11 the percentage of Americans viewing Islam positively has risen considerably.

Slow response to Bosnian crisis

Muslims throughout the world blame the West for the massacres and ethnic cleansing of Muslims, by the Serbians, that took place in Bosnia. They believe that Europeans did not want a Muslim country to be created in Europe. They are also convinced that if the victims had been non-Muslims, the reaction by the Western powers would have been considerably different and quicker.

The fact is that with some exceptions, American and other Western countries are loathe to undertake any military action, anywhere, that can cause them to lose soldiers unless economic necessity dictates it or there is a real threat to their national security. The guiding principle for America after the Vietnam War has been to avoid any engagement that requires it to commit troops unless a very clear objective, specific goals, and a timetable for withdrawal have been specified. Such requirements take time to be crystallized and, hence, even actions desired by the American administration are delayed. Such delays, to those who do not understand the engagement principles and process, can incorrectly indicate lack of interest.

Muslims also need to appreciate what happened in Kosovo, where the Serbs were bombarded and driven out by the Western powers. They need to realize that if the delayed response to the events in Bosnia had been driven by anti-Muslim feelings and considerations, the Western powers would not have taken military action in support of Muslims against the Serbs in Kosovo.

Most world Muslims are unaware, or unappreciative, of the fact that the American and Western governments were widely criticized by many prominent Western personalities and groups due to their slow reaction and failure to protect the Muslims in Bosnia. Among the most vocal critics of ethnic cleansing and Western delay in responding to the Bosnian crisis were Jews.

Guilty by association

In America, the development of anti-Muslim animosity can be traced to the rise of the Black Muslim movement and the hate and radicalism espoused by leaders such as Louis Farrakhan. Most Americans do not realize that the anti-Semitism and anti-white hatred preached by the Black Muslims is not supported by the basic tenets of Islam. Such hatred, which has disgusted and turned off most Americans, finds no sympathy or support among orthodox Muslims.

The radicalism of Malcolm X also disturbed most Americans. However, even though he realized that his beliefs were wrong and converted to mainstream Islam, which preaches race equality, the initial impression created by Malcolm X was too distasteful. Consequently, there has been a lasting negative impression, both of Malcolm X and the word *Muslim*, on the American population due to name association.

Muhammad Ali, the heavyweight boxing champion, cared for nonblacks even though most Americans believe otherwise. For example, he gave $100,000 to a home for the elderly in New York City, which was about to shut down due to financial problems, even though most of its inhabitants were Jews. Muhammad Ali, in order to promote his boxing fights in the 1970s, harped on the black superiority theme and highlighted black-white issues. He was very successful in his effort. However, he ended up being hated by most Americans due to draft-dodging and his white-baiting rhetoric even though he was not a racist at heart. Due to his rhetoric and association with Black Muslims, Americans also developed a very negative image of Islam and Muslims.

British influence and bias

The British, in contrast to Americans, have a history of working against Muslim interests, starting before the 1917 Balfour Declaration that resulted in the partition of Palestine. They have actively worked against Muslim countries including Turkey, Egypt, Palestine, Pakistan, Iraq, and Iran.

When India was partitioned in 1947, the British handed over Punjab's Gurdaspur district to India even though it had a Muslim majority and, according to partition rules, should have been made part of Pakistan. If Gurdaspur had been awarded to Pakistan, the Kashmir problem would never have existed because India would have had no common border with Kashmir. The transfer of Gurdaspur to India has been widely attributed by Pakistanis and Kashmiris to the hurt ego of Lord Mountbatten, the British governor general of undivided India. He wanted to get even with Pakistan because it had refused to make him its governor general after the partition, even though India had agreed to do so.

In 1951, Iran nationalized its oil industry and created the National Iranian Oil Company (NIOC). The Iranian action to become economically independent was vehemently opposed by Britain, which did not want to lose its tax revenues and control over Iran's oil resources. Western opposition, spearheaded by the British, led to the virtual collapse of Iran's oil industry and caused serious internal economic problems. In 1953, after the British got the Americans on board, a joint British-American operation was successfully executed to overthrow Dr. Mossadegh, the Iranian prime minister. Then in 1956, in disregard of international laws, Britain attacked Egypt when it reclaimed its sovereignty over the Suez Canal by nationalizing it.

Since the British have more experience in international affairs due to their colonial past, particularly in countries with large Muslim populations, they have often been followed, rather than led, by Americans. They have often set a hawkish tone and advised Americans to take a stance on various issues and crises that has not served either American or Muslim interests. For example, they laid the seeds of hatred against the West and America in Iran in 1951 when they tried to cripple the Iranian oil industry and, subsequently, presented a plan to the American government to overthrow the government of Dr. Mossadegh.

ANALYZING MUSLIM ISSUES AND FAILURES

Lack of education is widespread

Islam stresses education and encourages the quest for knowledge. The first injunction the Prophet Muhammad received from God was the verse, "Read in the name of your Lord Who created" (96.1). However, Muslims have not paid much attention to literacy and education in the past few centuries despite that injunction and other encouragement by the prophet, whose teachings they are required to follow.

For the majority of Muslims, especially in recent times, the main objective of becoming literate has been to read the Koran in Arabic. Therefore, the overwhelming majority of non-Arab Muslims are taught how to read Arabic without understanding its meaning. However, such an exercise has questionable benefits. The reason is that 78 percent of Muslims are non-Arab and therefore when they read the Koran in Arabic, they cannot understand what they are reading. Such "literacy" offers no practical and educational benefits in the secular world and neither does it enable such students to understand the teachings of Islam directly from the source (Koran).

In many parts of the world, Muslim girls are denied access to basic education, even where opportunities exist. Today, Muslim literacy rates are among the lowest in the world. With this weak foundation, it is not surprising that Muslims are economically disadvantaged in most parts of the world. Without good education, they cannot compete in the job market or avail themselves of opportunities that can improve their lot. While there are many socio-economic reasons and other external factors for their present condition, the ultimate blame for an uneducated community rests on the Muslims' own shoulders because they have not given education the importance it deserves.

Priorities are wrong

Human beings are required to make choices at every stage in their lives. In order to succeed, they need to prioritize and then make the best selection from among available choices. If choices are ranked correctly, the chances of consistent success are improved considerably. However, the requirement for prioritization is not limited to an individual's own choices. It extends to the community to which the individual belongs. For the overall success of a community, correct prioritization at both the personal and collective levels is a key requirement.

Muslims have not been good at prioritization. For too long, they have ignored important issues that should have been at the top of their list. For example, education has not been given high priority in recent memory. Neither has democracy and, along with it, accountability. Long-range and strategic options have ranked low because they do not produce immediate results. Focusing on the wrong issues due to incorrect prioritization has caused major problems for Muslims for centuries and has led to their decline in nearly every part of the world.

Religious extremists in control

Religious fundamentalists are usually very vocal and politically active. Many, such as some pro-lifers in America, become aggressive and use violence when they cannot get their way. Muslim fundamentalists are no different. They are frequently well organized and, quite often, create the impression that they are stronger in numbers than they actually are. In many countries, they are the only organized opposition to rulers who have reached, or retained, power through dubious means. Such rulers try to keep fundamentalists satisfied by acceding to their demands as long as their own power is not negatively impacted. For example, Pakistan is an Islamic country where religious parties have never managed to garner more than five percent of the seats in any national election. Despite that, they were able to pressure democratically elected Bhutto, a leftist non-religious Muslim who was quite popular, to pass religion-driven legislation in 1974 that declared the Ahmadiyya sect to be apostate and non-Muslim.

Even in moderate Muslim countries, religious fundamentalists hold considerable power despite lacking government authority, especially in the day-to-day affairs of the state. They try, and often succeed, in deriving authority from their righteous stance and moral high ground. Such people have honed their ability to use Islam as a tool for befuddling the common man, who often cannot separate these personalities from religion and, consequently, is unable to make an objective evaluation of religion-painted issues.

Historically, many Muslim rulers used the name of Islam while performing reprehensible acts for which there is no place in Islam. For example, Mahmud Ghazni invaded India 17 times between 1000 and 1025. He plundered its temples, famous for their wealth, including the well-known Somnath temple. While his barbarity was not restricted to non-Muslims, as exemplified by what he did to the Muslim ruler and people of Multan, his actions against the Hindus were against the tenets of Islam. His reprehensible actions earned Muslims the animosity of Hindus that persists even after one thousand years.

Religious extremists have often given a bad name to Islam, even in modern times, by mistreating, persecuting, or killing minorities. Islam clearly prohibits compulsion in religion. While the vast majority of Muslims are tolerant and get along with non-Muslim neighbors in all parts of the world, religious extremists have done Islam and other Muslims a great disservice by creating the impression that Muslims are intolerant.

Religion used as a cover to achieve ends

Since times immemorial, religion has been and continues to be a powerful tool for mobilizing and exploiting people in all parts of the world. Muslims are more susceptible to such mobilizing calls, which enjoin religious duty and obligation, due to their collective responsibilities specified by Islam. In too many cases, leaders in Muslim countries have put a religious cover on issues in order to obtain support they could not muster by using only secular merits.

The two most important struggles from the Muslims' perspective at this time are Palestine and Kashmir. Both of them started in regions that were characterized by religious tolerance. In both places, national liberation struggles were started and led for many years by secular nationalist organizations. However, in both cases, the leadership was ultimately taken over by parties that presented the resistance to occupation as an Islamic religious struggle against the Jews and Hindus. Despite the change in leadership, in both Palestine and Kashmir, secular parties continued their struggle to obtain freedom even though they were overshadowed.

In Palestine, Hamas, Islamic Jehad, and other religious groups were successful at presenting a genuine national liberation movement as a Muslim versus Jewish state struggle. Similarly, in Kashmir, the secular Jammu and Kashmir Liberation Front was displaced by a number of religious groups who managed to project the struggle against Indian occupation as a religious uprising against the Hindu oppressors. The reality is that even though Muslims are in an overwhelming majority in Kashmir, they have desired to regain their independence due to their history and nationalism rather than any animosity towards Hindus. In Kashmir, Muslims have lived peacefully for centuries with Pandits, who are high-caste Hindus.

The religious groups, in Palestine and Kashmir, have been very successful in mobilizing opposition to the Israelis and Indians. Ever since they took over the resistance, the cost of occupation for the Israelis and Indians has skyrocketed in terms of lives and money. However, the use of terrorism, especially in Israel, has also harmed the genuine liberation movements due to extremely negative press coverage in the West and also given Islam a bad name. The religious leaders, who fight in the name of a religion that condemns terrorism, should first have become well versed in their own religion before using it to achieve their objectives. The use of terror is clearly prohibited in Islam. It also does not justify illegal means to achieve a goal even if the objective is noble. Suicide bombing, which is a crime according to Islam, and especially the use of brainwashed teenagers for that strategy is something that every Muslim needs to condemn.

Palestine incorrectly portrayed as a religious struggle

The Palestinian struggle started out as a freedom movement led by nationalist Palestinians, both Muslims and Christians. Both al-Fatah and the Palestine Liberation Organization, which started active resistance against the Israeli occupation, were secular organizations. One of Israel's bitterest enemies, and the least compromising, has been Dr. George Habbash. He is a Christian leader who heads the Marxist Popular Front for the Liberation of Palestine (PFLP).

The Palestinian struggle first took a religious turn when part of the al-Aqsa Mosque was gutted in an arson attack by an Australian visitor two years after Israel occupied East Jerusalem. Also, as Arafat's failures became apparent and people lost faith in his ability to deliver, frustrated Palestinians looked elsewhere for leadership. Hamas, which had a social base and a record of community service, and other religious groups became popular and took on a leadership role in the resistance movement against the Israelis.

The Muslim error is that they have viewed the Palestinian struggle as an Islamic struggle, despite its being a national war of liberation, and mistakenly believed that the Palestinians were being oppressed due to their being Muslims. The fact is that both Christian and Muslim Palestinians have been oppressed and they both hate the Israelis equally. However, perception is reality. Consequently, Muslims believe that Palestinians are being subjected to suppression and humiliation just because they are Muslims. Therefore, it is not surprising that America, which has been supporting Israel unconditionally for decades, is associated with the oppression of Muslims.

Kuwait crisis was initiated by Iraq, not America

Many Muslims view the Gulf War and the pitting of Muslim coalition forces against Iraq as a conspiracy by America and the West to continue their scheme of making Muslim countries fight each other. They believe that the objective was to weaken Muslims as a follow-up to an earlier plot to drain the Iranians and Iraqis by making them fight each other for eight long years.

Unfortunately, Muslims who subscribe to this view conveniently forget the root cause of the problem—Saddam Hussein. He is among the worst, most evil men this world has ever seen. In addition to gassing his own people, he committed naked aggression against his neighbors, Iran and Kuwait. The two Iraqi-instigated wars left Iran and Iraq's economies in shambles, destroyed Kuwait's infrastructure, bled Saudi Arabia financially, devastated a generation of Iraqis and Iranians, and killed over a million Muslims.

Bhutto was responsible for his own downfall

The unfortunate fact is that the executed prime minister of Pakistan, Zulfikar Ali Bhutto, despite his brilliance, was power hungry and paranoid. Among his major crimes was his refusal to accept the results of the 1970 elections, in which his party came in second, that led to a bloody civil war and the ultimate breakup of Pakistan in 1971.

Bhutto was responsible for his own undoing. He rigged the Pakistani national elections in 1977. The common belief in Pakistan is that he would have won the elections, though with a smaller majority, even without the rigging. However, his paranoid nature forced him to manipulate the elections, which led to widespread street riots. The anti-Bhutto demonstrations and riots continued until the military, headed by General Zia-ul-Haq, dismissed Bhutto and took over.

Saudi non-oil exports have started creating major problems

The Saudi royal family's rule is considered by many Muslims to be un-Islamic because it violates the Islamic principle that a ruler should be elected through an elective process, which is ironic because of the royal family's self-appointed "Guardian of Islam" position. Both orthodox and radical Saudi Arabians question the religious legitimacy of the royal family and Saudi government. Therefore, as part of its effort to appear legitimate and cater to the sentiments of domestic religious fundamentalists, the Saudi royal family has run the country in a rigidly orthodox manner and initiated a program to export Islam.

The export program has involved funding religious extremist groups and madrassas in foreign countries. The products of that program are dogmatic, Wahhabi-type mullahs and religious zealots whose knowledge is limited to basic Islamic principles and teachings. Typically, such people lack secular education and their minds are closed to anything that appears materialistic or Western. A large number of Taliban soldiers were drawn from schools funded or supported by the Saudis.

The more recent Saudi export has been even more dangerous. A majority of the 19 hijackers who participated in the 9-11 atrocity were Saudis. If they had been nationals of any other country, the American government would have had a completely different attitude and reacted far more aggressively against that country. The American soft approach only confirms what is widely believed by Muslims—that America will do almost anything to ensure that the Saudis are not displeased because they control vast oil reserves.

Americans have failed to see the bigger picture of what the Saudi connection to 9-11 means and why so many Saudi nationals were involved in that attack. The event clearly indicates that there is very strong anti-American feeling even in friendly Saudi Arabia and, therefore, America should seriously analyze the causes for that sentiment and how it can be changed.

Poor communications and use of media

The media is a very powerful tool that can create, reinforce, or change views about almost any issue. One of the problems Muslims have been facing is their negative image that has been projected by the media in America, especially since 1973, due to a number of reasons and faults that can be attributed to both sides, as explained earlier.

The Israelis, using the media and their powerful lobby, succeeded in portraying Palestinians as Islamic terrorists many years before the first suicide bomber struck. India has also misled the world about Kashmir and its own record through a very effective public relations and media campaign. It has succeeded in focusing world attention on its "biggest" democracy and secularism, which project a positive image, while systematically and consistently killing Muslims in riots, occupying Kashmir by force since 1947, violating the human rights of Kashmiris and Sikhs, and even demolishing the historic Babri mosque. In March 2002, more than eight hundred Muslims were killed and thousands of their homes and businesses destroyed during an anti-Muslim pogrom in the Indian state of Gujarat. According to the Human Rights Watch report of April 30, 2002, Gujarat state officials were directly involved in those killings.

What Muslims lack is widespread projection of their side of the story using various media. This shortcoming has hurt them in the past and continues to do so now. While mastering media techniques, Muslims also need to ensure that their extremists are neutralized. They should not be allowed to project themselves as the spokesmen of the majority nor be allowed to carry out acts that, in the long run, harm the reputation and causes of Muslims worldwide. While the importance of positive media cannot be downplayed, Muslims should realize that even the most positive media coverage will not ultimately negate the effect of systematic criminal and terrorist acts perpetuated by a few using the name of Islam. Therefore, such elements should be completely marginalized.

Muslims lack role models

Over the centuries, many Muslims have been great role models for earlier Muslims. However, in the modern, fast-paced life of instant communications, there are very few Muslim role models. Role models, especially with national recognition, are lacking in politics, government, economics, medicine, law, social life, and sports.

Earlier role models, especially historical figures, can be used in the modern age in some ways, such as promoting characteristics and qualities that can be emulated at personal and family levels. However, there are few historical figures who can be related to modern issues. Muslims need new leadership models who can be looked up to from both religious and secular perspectives. They are needed at both national and personal levels. There is a dearth at the national level because Muslim leaders have let down their followers time and again. At the personal level, the lack of an educated community has limited the number of role models available to the Muslim community.

Majority is silent

The majority of Muslims throughout the world are silent and apathetic regarding what goes on outside their personal sphere. They are only interested in their day-to-day life, primarily due to economic and social circumstances. Consequently, the silence of the majority is misinterpreted and/or misrepresented. The most vocal Muslims are the radicals and extremists who, unfortunately, get maximum attention and media coverage. When the media focus on extremists and shows them shouting, "Death to America!" it appears that Muslims are thirsting for blood. What is not apparent or explained by the media is that such people represent less than five percent of Muslims. Osama bin Laden and other extremists are as representative of ordinary Muslims as the likes of David Koresh and the KKK represent Americans or the IRA represents Catholicism and the Pope. The Muslim silent majority, for whom the American way of life is a dream they would love to have rather than destroy, needs to shake off its current apathy and become more involved. Failure to do so will ensure that its representation will be in the hands of those whose actions have already done considerable harm.

Leadership has failed consistently

Muslim leadership has, by and large, been an abject failure in practically all parts of the world since the early days of Islam. Failure extends to political, economic, and religious leadership. Leadership failure has been an extremely important factor leading to the development of the conditions in which Muslims find themselves in at this time. It is quite apparent that unless Muslims produce better leaders, they cannot hope for a dramatic change in their existing condition. They need to realize that leaders, in most cases, are a reflection of the society at large. Therefore, unless Muslims instill good personal qualities within themselves and change for the better, their future leaders will continue to let them down.

Jehad hijacked

Muslims have let jehad be hijacked by both Muslims and non-Muslims. For centuries they have viewed many conflicts as jehad, even though they were not, by allowing themselves to be misled by Muslims who had selfish and wrong agendas and objectives. The two primary reasons for their being led astray are emotions and ignorance regarding jehad. Muslims share the blame for the negative perception of jehad among non-Muslims, especially in America, because they have failed to counter misinformation and misinterpretation regarding jehad. Their passive attitude has contributed to the perception that they are associated with an intolerant and aggressive religion.

On the other hand, Western media have helped paint an incorrect picture of jehad and what it stands for. Most of the media usually have simply reported the exhortation of Muslim extremists, urging jehad, without presenting adequate additional information about an emotional and hot topic as required by good journalism standards. In the past, such collateral information would have clearly shown that many of those issuing the jehad calls were misrepresenting Islam for their own criminal agendas. Though many recent articles and news stories have accurately reported the primary objective of jehad, which means a personal inner struggle, and how ordinary Muslims view it, the timely lack of such information has contributed to its very negative perception in the eyes of Americans.

CHAPTER 6

FAILURE OF MUSLIM LEADERSHIP

The decline of Islamic power and the plight of Muslims, especially in the 20th century, have many causes directly attributable to Muslims. While some blame can be assigned to individuals, a significant amount of responsibility can be attributed to failed Muslim leaders. Many of them led their countries on the path of destruction—politically, economically, and socially. In many cases, countries ready to become powerhouses ended in disarray due to corruption, mismanagement, and misrule by despots, dictators, and incompetent rulers. The following sections list some of the worst Muslim leadership failures, political and religious, in the modern age.

POLITICAL LEADERSHIP

Organization of Islamic Conference

After an attempt was made in 1969 to burn down the al-Aqsa mosque, located in Israeli-controlled Jerusalem, Muslim countries got together and created an organization called the Organization of Islamic

Conference (OIC). The primary objective of the OIC was to unite Muslims. However, all it has succeeded in doing is organize annual conferences where the leaders of the member countries meet and issue statements. In more than three decades, the OIC has yet to produce anything practical or meaningful.

The OIC leadership is, by and large, composed of national leaders who do not represent the will and aspirations of their people. Most of the leaders have either not been elected or they won in elections that were not free. Most of them have risen to leadership positions through manipulation, deceit, heredity, military coups, questionable elections, and other dubious means—all un-Islamic practices.

Genuine leaders have to rise and be accepted and respected by the population at large before they can be truly representative. Only when that happens can a toothless organization like the OIC have the moral authority to lead and make decisions. For that to happen, Muslims should not look to America or the West because they respect democracy or are powerful. Instead, they should accept their own responsibility and take appropriate steps for achieving democracy within their own countries.

Arabs

The Arab world has had more than its share of dictators and despots, and they continue coming in an endless parade. It is not unusual for a feared, detested, or incompetent ruler to be followed by an even worse one. The brutality of some of these leaders, their suppression of their own populations, and making their neighbors live in fear are completely un-Islamic.

The worst modern Arab ruler is Saddam Hussein, whose character is well known. What is regrettable is that a large number of Muslims sympathize with him. What they forget or are ignorant of is the fact that Saddam is responsible for more Muslim deaths, resulting from the Iran-Iraq war he started, than anyone else in history except Stalin.

Hosni Mubarak of Egypt, who runs a corrupt and inefficient administration that has not uplifted the life of the Egyptian masses despite billions in American aid and loan write-offs, is out of touch with the feelings and aspirations of his people.

Hafez Assad of Syria was another brutal dictator. His troops systematically massacred more than ten thousand men, women, and children over a period of weeks in the town of Hama, which was sympathetic to the opposition.

Kaddafi is another dictator who has kept himself in power for more than 30 years. His misrule had practically ruined Libya's economy, despite its vast oil resources, even before the economic embargo was imposed due to the bombing of Pan Am 103 over the Scottish town of Lockerbie in 1988.

Iran

Iran, an oil-rich country, has had two major leaders in the past half century. The Shah of Iran, a Sunni, ruled the country until the Khomeni-led revolution overthrew him in 1979. While the country did make good economic progress during the Shah's tenure, fueled by massive oil revenues, wealth distribution was very inequitable. The Shah also suppressed the Shias, who accounted for 80 percent of the population, and anyone else who dared oppose him. Torture of opponents by the feared SAVAK, the secret police, was widespread during his reign. When the people finally rose against him, the Shah had no choice but to flee.

Ayatollah Khomeni returned to Iran from exile in France in 1979. He was a spiritual leader who let the country be run by other politically motivated ayatollahs. The new dogmatic rulers, with their hardline, medieval views, succeeded in ruining an economy that had been quite vibrant. During their rule of more than two decades, the Iranian economy has struggled. Opposition has been stifled and human rights have been violated even though Islam guarantees them. Additionally, the condition of women has gone from bad to worse under the rule of the ayatollahs. After the revolution, the family protection law was abrogated which effectively denied women the right to divorce. Women were restricted from certain professions (such as law) and university programs (such as agricultural engineering and veterinary sciences), barred from being judges, and required to obtain the permission of the father or husband in order to travel abroad.

Pakistan

Pakistan was a country of hard-working people that was born with great dreams, after great sacrifices, in 1947. It had vast potential and initially made good progress. However, in the past three decades, three powerful leaders have failed it miserably. That this Islamic country is still intact after all it has gone through in the past half century is nothing short of a miracle.

Zulfikar Ali Bhutto, Zia-ul-Haq, and Nawaz Sharif either had comfortable parliamentary majorities or the backing of the powerful military while they were in authority. They were extremely powerful and could practically rule by decree. As is well documented in government white papers, judicial records, newspaper reports, and human rights reports issued by various organizations, all three were responsible for many abuses and crimes.

The three leaders rigged elections, made corruption a part of daily life, killed political opponents, patronized generals who smuggled drugs, made a mockery of the justice system and its judges, humiliated the figurehead president, introduced guns into the society, bought state industries at fire-sale prices in the name of privatization, used sectarian extremists to kill innocent people, murdered religious minorities, etc. Each one of these is a major crime according to Islam, which is the official religion of Pakistan.

Unfortunately, Pakistanis tend to blame other countries, especially the West, for their mess rather than lay the blame squarely where it lies—third-rate leaders who left the country in political and economic chaos. The inability to acknowledge that the fault can be their own is common among Muslims.

Indonesia

Indonesia is the most populous Muslim country in the world. It had great economic potential after it became an independent country in 1949 after more than three centuries of Dutch colonial rule. After independence, two of its rulers, Sukarno and Suharto, reigned over Indonesia for decades. However, both of them were failures.

When Sukarno was forced to leave after a failed communist coup attempt in 1965, the country was polarized and came close to economic ruin. Suharto, who followed him, also turned out to be an incompetent ruler. His rule was characterized by failed policies, corruption, cronyism, and nepotism that caused the country, which had the potential to be an Asian powerhouse, immense economic harm. On the religious and political front, Indonesia's 1975 occupation and subsequent ruthless suppression of Catholic-majority East Timor has contributed to the perception that Islam is intolerant.

Revolutionary: Algeria and Afghanistan

It has been the misfortune of Muslims in modern times that whenever they got rid of a dictator or an occupying power, the replacement often turned out to be equally bad or even worse. After Algeria won its freedom from the French, following an armed struggle characterized by tremendous suffering and sacrifice, its new local rulers let the country down. In the new setup, democracy was denied and the Algerian rulers ruined the economy despite abundant oil reserves. For more than a decade the country has been wrecked by civil war. It started when the army prevented the Islamic Salvation Front, which easily won the first-round of elections, from coming to power by canceling the second-round elections. The civil war, which has been extremely brutal and dirty, has killed tens of thousands of innocent people.

After the Afghan mujahideen defeated the Soviet army, their own tribal rivalries came to the forefront. The result was a vicious civil war, even more destructive than the war against the Soviets, that destroyed Afghanistan economically, politically, and socially. More people have been killed in the post-Soviet civil war than were killed in the war against the communists. The civil war also led to an anarchic situation in which the Taliban came to power. They ruled with an iron hand and implemented rules, especially for women, which were backward even by Afghan standards. On the political level, they made the mistake of allowing Osama bin Laden to establish terrorist bases in Afghanistan. The result has been even more destruction, at the hands of Americans, following the 9-11 attack.

RELIGIOUS LEADERSHIP

Saudi Arabia

Saudi Arabian rulers are the custodians of the Kaaba in the city of Mecca. They are viewed as the spiritual leaders of world Muslims, who look to them for moral leadership. However, except for Feisal, Saudi kings have failed miserably to provide leadership to the Muslim world. Their stand on world issues has rarely reflected the views and aspirations of average Muslims.

Un-Islamic activities in Saudi Arabia have caused considerable harm to the reputation of the Saudi royal family. Alcohol is easily available to the royal family and those with the right connections, even though it is strictly prohibited by Islam. Civil and criminal laws are not uniformly applied to Saudi citizens and non-citizens. It is not unusual for a Saudi to be let off while, for the same crime, an expatriate Muslim is awarded the maximum sentence and, in many cases, deported. This flouts

Islamic law, its concept of justice, and what the Prophet Muhammad preached in his last sermon—that all people are equal.

Instead of providing religious and moral leadership at the national level, where it is needed, the Saudis have deemed it more appropriate to provide it at the grassroots level. However, their view regarding what should be exported is not in sync with the rest of the Islamic world, which does not agree with the dogmatic beliefs of the Saudis. Saudis follow the rigid and puritanical Wahhabi sect that interprets Islam in a way that is not acceptable to the overwhelming majority of Muslims.

The Saudis have tried to provide leadership to the Islamic world in their own unique way. They have been exporting their brand of Islam by funding organizations that turn out rigid clones and dogmatic Taliban types through madrassas. At such institutions, students are taught by teachers uneducated in non-Islamic subjects. They also do not provide secular and balanced education, which is required for success in the modern world. This leadership method has failed as has been shown by the end result in Afghanistan.

Iran

The Iran-Iraq war of the 1980s continued for eight bloody years. Except at the beginning, when one side had the upper hand and a counterattack succeeded, front-line positions were fairly static within a narrow war zone near the border. Because Ayatollah Khomeni believed Iran was in the morally right position and he expected ultimate victory, he refused to end the war. When he finally realized an outright victory was not possible, Khomeni agreed to end the war, and peace descended on two war-weary nations. However, it arrived only after a devastating loss of life, estimated to be more than a million, and severe economic damage to both countries.

The Iran-Iraq war could have been brought to a close years earlier. The failure of both countries, and Iran in particular, to negotiate an earlier end to the war has had a very detrimental impact on the political and economic situation in the Persian Gulf area. The war led to the two largest Muslim countries in the region being set back economically at least 20 years. Politically, it created enmity that will persist for generations.

World

Religious leadership in most countries with large, or majority, Muslim populations is practically nonexistent. Political leadership in such countries is usually completely separate from religious leadership. Typically, political leaders are secular and do not carry any weight in religious affairs.

The activities of the religious leadership are confined to mosques and religious schools. Their most important tasks include leading daily ritual prayers and the Friday congregational prayer. A few scholarly leaders also issue Islamic rulings on issues confronting Muslims. However, many religious leaders hardly know the religion, other than its basic rituals, and cannot be expected to provide real leadership.

Muslim religious parties with political aspirations do exist in many countries. Typically, such parties are ultraconservative and do not command the allegiance of more than 5 to 10 percent of the population. Despite their appeal to religious feelings, they lack popularity because the majority of people prefer candidates who they think can provide them with the basic necessities of life. This is a common theme throughout the world and is best exemplified by the phrase, "It's the economy, stupid!"

America

American Muslims are among the most highly educated Muslims in the world. Their community includes many learned religious scholars who have made their mark in both the secular and religious worlds. They have an excellent opportunity to create a community, that can be a model for Muslims all over the world, in a country that affords many opportunities and permits religious freedom. American Muslim leaders have not yet succeeded because they have been unable to unite.

Some Muslim communities with dedicated members have done highly commendable work. However, politics, leadership battles, infighting, lack of or limited democracy, ethnic issues, and a host of other problems plague many Muslim communities and Islamic centers. American Muslim leaders, most of them immigrants, are more interested in personal status and position, which they tend to inflate through the size of their mosques, than in providing service to the community outside their mosques. Many of these centers, instead of being independent, appear to be under the influence of the Saudis.

American-born Muslim leaders have yet to make their mark though a few have great potential, including Hamza Yusuf (Mark Hanson). A white American who converted to Islam, Hamza is charismatic, a brilliant orator, and a highly accomplished Islamic scholar who speaks Arabic fluently. He has become one of the most respected American Muslim religious leaders. Before meeting with President Bush in the White House on September 20, 2001, he said, "Islam was hijacked on that plane as an innocent victim."

Unfortunately, instead of building through a positive approach, Hamza initially harangued against Jews and practically everything American during his khutbas (Friday sermons). He would put down leading American universities, characterizing them as Jewish, and advise his audience to stay away from such institutions. Youth are impressionable, and his negative impact on them has been apparent for some time. According to a February 15, 2002, article in the *Wall Street Journal*, Hamza has toned down his rhetoric and modified his views. Hamza's acknowledgement of his mistakes and modified views is a welcome sign because it shows that he has the courage to acknowledge his mistakes, a characteristic that has been somewhat lacking in Muslim leaders. Muslims need leaders like him who have the capability to influence Muslim youth, the future leaders who can help show Americans what Islam is really like and end the stereotyping of Muslims. They need to support leaders such as Hamza who can build bridges between Muslims and America.

CHAPTER 7

JEHAD HIJACKED

The invocation of the word *jehad* conjures up different images, depending on whether the person is a Muslim or a non-Muslim, because it has been misinterpreted and maligned for centuries. For non-Muslims, it brings up images of war-mongering Muslims bent upon forcibly converting non-Muslims to Islam. For Americans, it brings up images of bin Laden advocating jehad and, consequently, images of an attack on civilian targets and government. For a few Muslims, the cry of "Jehad" is a call to take up arms to protect Islam and Muslims. For ignorant extremist Muslims, whose numbers are insignificant, it means the subjugation of non-Muslims. However, for those who know and understand Islam, jehad has a far different objective that has nothing to do with violence and war, except in exceptional circumstances.

VIOLENCE, COMPULSION, AND WAR

Does Islam preach violence

Islam does not preach violence. It prohibits forced conversions or the use of force against innocent or unarmed people. It does not allow violence to be used for spreading Islam. Islam also prohibits the destruction of property. However, it does allow self-defense or the taking up of arms against aggressors. The Koran says, "Fight in the way of Allah against those who fight against you, but begin not hostilities. Lo! Allah loveth not aggressors" (2:190).

In recent years, some of the most high-profile terrorist acts in the world that have impacted Americans have involved Muslims. They include the Lockerbie Pan Am bombing, World Trade Center bombing in 1993, and the attack of September 11, 2001. These acts helped create the perception that Muslims are violent and intolerant extremists. What has not helped is the stereotyping by some in the American media who have chosen to blame Muslims and/or Islam rather than the specific perpetrating groups and individuals whose actions were in contradiction of the tenets of Islam.

The Muslims' stereotypical image of intolerant and aggressive religious zealots, creating fear among non-believers, is far from reality. A very small group of Muslims do subscribe to extremist views, just as some followers of other religions do, but they do not represent the vast majority of Muslims. Their beliefs also do not reflect the teachings of Islam—especially concerning violence. Extremists and terrorists represent Islam and Muslims as much as David Koresh, who used the Bible to justify his actions, represented Christianity. Similarly, Saddam Hussein and Osama bin Laden represent Islam as much as Adolf Hitler and Timothy McVeigh represent Christianity.

The fact that Islam is neither violent nor extreme is well recognized now. President Bush and many other American leaders have stressed this fact, which has done a lot to promote understanding and remove misconceptions. It also earned considerable respect for President Bush among Muslims for stating this forcefully at a very critical time for America when emotions were running high.

Is Islam tolerant

According to Islam, acceptance of God and the performance of His worship must be of one's free will. As a consequence, Islam guarantees freedom of belief. According to the Koran, "There is no compulsion in religion." If someone is coerced into accepting Islam, such acceptance becomes worthless because there can be no sincere conversion without free will.

Islam preaches that minorities and their places of worship must be protected. It allows non-Muslims to run their own courts for implementing family law. The following examples illustrate how Muslims practiced Islam when its teachings were being implemented correctly:

- Muhammad forbade the destruction of Christian and Jewish places of worship.
- Umar, the second caliph, refused to pray inside a Christian church in Jerusalem when Muslims conquered it. He did not want them to consider his action as a tradition and, subsequently, insist that Muslims pray inside the church or convert it into a mosque.
- Jews as well as other non-Muslims flourished under Muslim rule in Spain, which lasted for eight hundred years.
- Muslim dynasties ruled over India for more than six centuries and, yet, Hinduism remains the religion of 81 percent of its population.

Freedom of religion granted to minorities led to Christians and Jews supporting, as well as welcoming, Muslim rule in many places. In 641, it was the archbishop of the Egyptian Coptic Church who requested Muslims to get rid of the Romans. Despite Muslim rule for centuries over vast areas with large Christian minorities, they continued to flourish, especially during the Golden Age of Islam. If Muslims had been as intolerant as Isabella of Spain, no Christians or Jews would have survived under their rule.

Islam was also absorbed easily in most countries because it did not seek to impose radical cultural change. An important factor in its success was allowing regional identities to remain distinct. This can be observed in the differences among Muslims ranging from Libya to Indonesia and from Europe to America.

Perception of Islamic intolerance: a disconnect

There is a common perception among non-Muslims, especially in the West, that Islam is an intolerant religion and that it spread by the sword. While it is true that Muslims made many conquests during their initial expansion, most of them were for restoring freedoms and getting rid of oppressors. During those expeditions, Muslims were driven by the zeal to spread the word of God. However, they did not force local populations to convert to Islam. Much later, some misguided rulers did force conversions in contravention of the injunction in the Koran, "There is no compulsion in religion" (2:256). The spread of Islam through such means was insignificant. However, it helped create the perception that Islam is intolerant even though it opposes any forced conversions.

Some of the most feared rulers of their times, such as the Mongols' Genghis Khan and his grandson Halagu, wrought death and destruction over vast areas. Their names are associated with brutality, massacres, and intolerance. Many of them, including Halagu, first defeated Muslim countries or dynasties but subsequently converted to Islam. Through association, Islam is also perceived negatively due to acts committed by feared historical figures such as Halagu before their conversion to Islam.

Another reason for the belief that Muslims spread Islam by the sword is lack of knowledge. For example, Genghis Khan is mistakenly believed to be a Muslim, by both Muslims and non-Muslims, due to his last name—a common Muslim surname at this time.

Over the years, due to constant repetition, the myth of suppression and forced conversions by Muslims has taken hold. One region in particular where Muslims have been severely taken to task is the Indian subcontinent. India was ruled by Muslim dynasties for more than six hundred years, while the very powerful Mughals ruled with an iron hand for more than three hundred years. The Mughal kings frequently married Rajput Hindu women and were extremely tolerant, with the exception of Aurangzeb. Despite Islamic rule over India for six centuries, its Muslim population is barely 12 percent. The numbers speak for themselves. A factor in the negative image of Muslims in India is the death and destruction caused by Tamerlane, a Muslim, in 1398 when he sacked Delhi and killed one hundred thousand people. A frequently ignored fact is that India was ruled at that time by a Muslim belonging to the Tughlaq dynasty.

In Kashmir, where the Muslim population of the valley is 95 percent, King Rainchan and his queen followed different religions—Hinduism and Buddhism—and could not decide which of them should convert. In 1314, they decided to resolve the issue by adopting the religion of the first person whose voice they would hear the next morning. At dawn the next day, they heard the Muslim call to prayer and decided to convert to Islam. Following tradition, their subjects also converted to Islam.

When Muslims defeated the Byzantines and others, they did not forcibly convert anyone. Instead, the local people's contact with the Muslims often led to their conversion to Islam. In the Golden Age of Islam, Christians and Jews were extremely well treated. Often, during the period of the Islamic Empire, Jewish minorities fled to Muslim countries to escape persecution from Christians. Jews returned to Jerusalem after Salahuddin defeated the Crusaders and retook Jerusalem. The following points also refute the claim that Islam was mostly spread by force:

- Muslim merchants spread Islam along ancient trade routes. Countries converted in this way include Indonesia, the largest Muslim country, which never saw the arrival of Muslim armies.
- In America, millions have converted to Islam through peaceful means.

On the other hand, excesses against Muslims have not been infrequent. Some examples of either complete or partial annihilation and expulsions carried out in Europe include Spain after the end of Muslim rule, Sicily, Greece, Russia during Stalin's rule, Chechnya, and the Balkans.

Why Muslim tolerance has declined

Muslim tolerance has declined considerably since the early days of Islam. It is an irony that tolerance among Muslims has decreased as they strayed from their religion. The more they strayed, the more intolerant they became in violation of their own religious beliefs and teachings. In contrast, the West has become more tolerant the more it has distanced itself from religion, which had been associated with intolerance and persecution.

Forced conversions made under Islamic rule were done against the teachings of Islam. However, such acts of intolerance have not been any different, or more frequent, than those perpetuated by Christians or others in the past. It must be recognized that intolerance and persecution carried out by anyone, Muslim or non-Muslim, does not make that person's religion guilty, especially if the faith prohibits intolerance and forced conversions clearly and without caveats.

When Islam permits war

Islam permits a Muslim to take up arms for a number of reasons, including self-defense, defending the religion, defense of basic human rights, persecution, or if forced from his home. It allows a life to be risked for a righteous cause, even though life is considered sacred, in order to prevent injustice from being triumphant.

Islam permits hostility against those who practice oppression but not against those who refrain from aggression. War is viewed as the last option and can only be fought under certain rules. Islam lays down strict rules of combat which include prohibitions against:
- Harming civilians
- Destroying property, crops, trees, and livestock
- Continuing fighting if the enemy seeks peace
- Committing treachery
- Mutilating dead bodies
- Exceeding bounds (restriction that any retaliation cannot exceed the originally perpetrated injustice)

JEHAD

Concept and purpose of jehad

The word *jehad* is derived from the Arabic *jahada*, which means to struggle. In practical terms, jehad means constant striving to achieve righteousness and justice through all means, including spiritual, moral, and material. In extreme cases, it can be invoked to take up arms and risk one's life for a cause such as the defense of Islam. However, the greatest and most common jehad, which is also the most difficult, is the struggle with one's self.

The following are examples of actions that can be considered jehad:
- Attempting to put God, whom one cannot see, ahead of everyday life and issues such as family, job, desires, pursuit of wealth and success, social life, society, etc.
- Resisting pressure from family, friends, and society to act or live in a way that does not please God

- Personal struggle with one's self
- Making an effort to wake up for the mandatory early morning prayer
- Trying to be virtuous and fighting temptations
- Attempting to submit to God in various aspects of life
- Practicing religion in the face of oppression and persecution
- Resisting injustice
- Standing up against unjust laws or a dictator
- Speaking the truth even though the boss may not like it
- Ordinary, but difficult, acts such as trying to quit smoking or controlling one's temper
- Serving parents

The following actions do not constitute jehad:
- Terrorizing minorities or civilians
- Fighting for land or nationalism
- Fighting for power
- Fighting for wealth, honor, or revenge
- Fighting to force others to accept Islam
- Fighting against evil by using violence
- Making jehad a tool of oppression

Misconception about jehad

Jehad is primarily a personal struggle against one's inner self and not a holy war against non-Muslims or a tool of oppression and forced conversions. However, the common perception among non-Muslims is that it means "Holy War," or a declaration of war against infidels. Its invocation creates fear and images of violence and forced conversions at the point of the sword. This perception is completely divorced from reality and does not represent what Islam teaches about jehad.

Both Muslims and the Western media are to be blamed for the incorrect perception about jehad. Muslims have used the term incorrectly and casually—applying it to situations that have nothing to do with jehad. The Western media has failed, while reporting on jehad, to present its true perspective. The term has also been misapplied and hijacked by terrorists. While the war in Afghanistan from 1979 to 1989 could be termed a true jehad, which is what made it well-known to Americans to start with, its subsequent application by terrorists like bin Laden is a travesty of the concept of jehad.

When war or armed action can be justified as jehad

The struggle against one's inner self is referred to as the "greater jehad." The struggle against outside forces, which involves the taking up of arms, is referred to as the "lesser jehad." Islam allows Muslims to take up arms under the jehad banner for a number of reasons including:
- Self-defense
- Struggle against tyranny, exploitation, and oppression; can be against Muslims or non-Muslims
- Defense of one's own country
- Defense of Islam or a Muslim country (such as Afghanistan which had been invaded by the Soviets, and its citizens were being killed indiscriminately, even though it had not threatened any of its neighbors)

Unholy wars

The term *Holy War* is a foreign concept to Islam. The term was coined by the Christians during the Crusades and has no basis in Islam. Wars, in the name of Islam or by Muslims, to grab territories, oppress, or forcibly convert non-Muslims can be classified as unholy wars because they have no Islamic sanction.

Over the centuries, rulers in all parts of the world have waged wars for expanding territories, increasing personal power, spreading religion, gaining honor and fame, increasing wealth and accumulating riches, etc. Such rulers have been associated with all religions, including Islam and Christianity. In many cases, Muslim rulers used Islam or jehad as a rallying cry to obtain support for wars that violated Islamic principles or had questionable motives that had no relevance to Islam or jehad. In the view of Islam, such wars were wrong and cannot even be justified, much less classified as jehads.

TERRORISM

Islamic view of terrorism

The objective of terrorism is to target civilians in order to create fear in a society. Since such an objective is in conflict with clearly stated Islamic principles, true Islam cannot support terrorism. The Islamic view of terrorism has been clearly stated in the Koran and also by Prophet Muhammad. According to the Koran, the taking of one innocent life is equivalent to the killing of all mankind.

If a person commits an act of terrorism, it does not negate or change the principles of the religion he claims to follow. If a Catholic IRA terrorist detonates a bomb in London, it does not mean that Catholicism supports or encourages terrorism. Similarly, if a Muslim commits an act of terror, it does not mean that Islam condones or encourages terrorism.

Many terrorists are part of genuine liberation movements. However, even though the perpetrators of terrorism may have genuine goals, such as liberating their country from oppression or an occupying power, the Islamic view of their actions is based upon the following principles:
- Illegal means cannot be used to justify the end result
- Acts of terrorism that harm innocent people are prohibited
- Attacking occupation forces is acceptable

Both state-sponsored and individual acts of terrorism are un-Islamic

Terrorism can be committed by an individual or by a country. However, the word *terrorism* these days usually refers to acts of terrorism by individuals or small groups. According to Islam, terrorism is wrong whether it is committed by:
- An individual
- A group
- A state

According to Islamic principles, all the actions in the following list are wrong because they can be classified as terrorist acts:
- Saddam Hussein's chemical attack on Kurd villages
- Bombing civilian areas during wartime
- Muslim governments terrorizing Christian minorities in Sudan and East Timor
- Suicide bombing of the World Trade Center
- Army killing of civilians in Hama, Syria
- Blowing up of a passenger bus by a suicide bomber in Israel
- Indiscriminate demolition of civilian homes and the killing of civilians by Israel in Jenin, Palestine
- Israeli soldiers killing stone-throwing Palestinian children demanding an end to occupation
- Indian army's routine retaliatory burning of shopping centers and homes in Kashmir
- Deliberate destruction of towns and villages in Chechnya by the Russians
- Sudanese government's bombing of civilian and humanitarian targets in southern and central Sudan
- Burning of crosses by the KKK
- Killing fellow workers in a post office

❑ Bombing an abortion clinic, even though Islam prohibits abortion

No one has a monopoly on terrorism. Both individuals and states carry it out throughout the world. It is implemented in the name of religion, national interest, personal belief, racial superiority, etc. The practice of terrorism is not restricted to the so-called rogue states or small groups. It is also perpetuated by mainstream countries. Some have terrorized the citizens of countries they have occupied, such as Palestine and Kashmir, for decades. The Islamic view is that all types of terrorism are wrong, whether they are committed by an individual or by a state.

Suicide bombing and martyrdom

A soldier in a war can be very brave and take many risks. So long as there is a chance of surviving, a soldier's life-jeopardizing actions are not considered wrong by Islam. In every society, Muslim and non-Muslim, an extremely brave soldier's actions are glorified because he places his own life at considerable risk in order to achieve an objective. However, a suicide bomber falls in a different category.

A suicide bomber undertakes a task knowing that it will lead to certain death. In other words, such a person undertakes to commit suicide in order to achieve a specific objective. According to Islam, suicide is one of the worst possible sins. Recently, suicide bombers have been referred to as martyrs. However, Islam considers a person to be a martyr only if he is killed while fighting against evil or defending Islam. A suicide bomber, instead of being killed by someone, kills himself. Therefore, such a person cannot be referred to as a martyr. Unfortunately, many young, uninformed and frustrated Palestinian Muslims have been lured into thinking that they will become martyrs and go to heaven if they commit suicide.

Is Islam responsible for terrorism carried out in its name

In recent times, Islam has been blamed for acts of terrorism carried out in its name, even though such acts were against Islamic principles. While it is true that Muslim terrorist organizations have carried out many acts of terrorism in recent years, it should be noted that many non-Muslim terrorist organizations, including the Basque ETA and the IRA, have also been very active. One of the earliest terrorist organizations in the Middle East was the Irgun Zvai Leumi, a Jewish organization that was very active in Palestine from 1931 to 1948.

The following points should be kept in mind when attempting to relate Islam to terrorism:
- Islam considers all terrorism acts to be wrong without exception.
- Catholics and Christians have been pioneers in modern terrorism, even before the Black September Palestinian group made world headlines in the 1970s. The four oldest terrorist organizations in the world are the Catholic ETA (Basque-Spain), Catholic IRA (Ireland), Christian Nagas (India), and Christian Mizos (India), all of whom have been routinely conducting terrorist bombings and killings for three or four decades.
- Every Palestinian bombing or terrorist act is classified as Islamic even though Christian Arabs are also actively resisting the Israelis.
- The Irgun, a Jewish terrorist organization, blew up Jerusalem's King George hotel, killing 90 people, in 1946. In 1948, it participated in the massacre at Dier Yassin village where 250 civilians were systematically murdered. Menachem Begin, the ex-prime minister of Israel, was an Irgun leader.

No religion, including Islam or Catholicism, should be blamed and held responsible for acts of terrorism carried out in its name. Terrorism is a crime against humanity and no religion should be associated with it, despite what the perpetrators say, because none sanctions it.

FUNDAMENTALISM

What is fundamentalism

These days, a person is usually considered to be a fundamentalist if he belongs to the most conservative wing of his religion. Some people label as fundamentalists those Christians who are opposed to abortion, homosexuality, physician-assisted suicide, sex education in schools, etc. Among Christians, however, fundamentalism refers to the rigidity with which a group imposes its beliefs and interpretations of the scripture on others. Islamic fundamentalism can be defined based on the degree of conservatism or liberalism of its followers. However, Islamic fundamentalism is being incorrectly associated with extremists and terrorists who violate its principles rather than follow it.

A conservative, or fundamentalist, uses his religion as a model for guiding and living his life in the modern world. In contrast, an extremist uses violence and terrorism to achieve his objectives. Extremists may or may not be religious fundamentalists though they often are in the case of Muslims. A distinction must be made between a fundamentalist and an extremist. There are many Islamic fundamentalists all over the world whose fundamentalism is limited to their routine daily lives and religious rituals, but the percentage of Muslim extremists is very low. However, in some areas such as the Middle East, they have considerable strength and pose a definite threat to Israel and America.

What Islamic fundamentalism represents

The true fundamentalists in Islam and Christianity are the ones who desire a return to basic traditional values and practices. They want their followers to be sheltered from the ills of modern life such as immorality, immodesty, homosexuality, disrespect for parents, materialism, etc. Islamic fundamentalists also desire the implementation of rule by Sharia in Muslim majority countries. The overwhelming majority of

Islamic fundamentalists are pious people who respect traditional values and are not in conflict with the Koranic teachings of tolerance and moderation.

A true Muslim is a fundamentalist so far as the practice of the religion is concerned. A person who truly follows religious teachings cannot be an extremist because Islam prohibits violence and terrorism while teaching moderation and tolerance.

Who and where are the Muslim fundamentalists

Most Middle Eastern terrorists appear to be fundamentalist Muslims so far as the daily practice of their religion is concerned. However, they share little with fundamentalists who are religious conservatives. Terrorists represent a radical wing that believes in achieving objectives through violence. Their objectives can be quite varied, including creating an Islamic state, freeing a country from occupation, overthrowing a secular government, implementing rule by Sharia, etc.

The extremist fundamentalist movement is fueled by social, religious, and economic conditions in many Muslim countries. They include lack of democracy and human rights, restricted personal freedom and fundamental rights, autocratic and unelected political leadership, refugee life, inequitable distribution of wealth, widespread poverty, lack of education, high unemployment, and lack of justice.

What has swelled the ranks of fundamentalists

There are a number of reasons why more and more Muslims have turned to fundamentalism, and in some cases to extremism and terrorism, in the past two decades. They include:
- Economic failure of Muslim countries and inability to provide jobs for their youth
- Corruption and injustice in many Muslim societies
- Worsening situation of Muslims worldwide
- Call for jehad against the Soviets during the war in Afghanistan

- Crises in Palestine, Bosnia, Kosovo, Iraq, Kashmir, and Chechnya
- Iranian revolution
- Worsening Saudi economy and the presence of American troops in Saudi Arabia
- Resurgence of Islam in many countries

CHAPTER 8

BUILDING A BETTER FUTURE

WHAT WORLD MUSLIMS NEED TO DO

Address root causes of problems

In order to improve their overall condition and status, Muslims need to identify the root causes of problems afflicting them by thoroughly analyzing their issues. It is essential that the diagnosis be accurate because addressing symptoms, rather than causes, will not achieve anything meaningful. Once root causes are identified and solved, minor problems will fade away. The approach must be disciplined, which is counter to the tendency to implement solutions that show results in a shorter time and have more political capital associated with them.

Prioritize correctly

Resource limitations and other conditions significantly influence when and how communities resolve problems. They force prioritization that determines the sequence in which problems are addressed, based on their relative importance to the community. The degree of success that will be achieved by Muslims in addressing their problems will depend upon their approach and how they prioritize their issues. In theory, the prioritization task appears to be quite easy. In practice, it is difficult because there is no unity among Muslims and, consequently, prioritization becomes an uphill task. However, each country can prioritize independently and use the results to solve its own problems. Later, after achieving success, it can become a model for other countries which failed to prioritize correctly.

Recognize Israel

The Arab-Israeli issue is one of the root causes of problems that Muslims have with America and the West. The conflict has diverted their resources, drained them emotionally, and prevented much needed economic development. While it is recognized that Arabs suffered injustice when Israel was created, Muslims need to move forward. There can be no turning back of the clock. They should make a serious effort to resolve the Arab-Israeli conflict. They must negotiate with Israel in good faith, just as the Israelis must, and make it clear that they will provide Israel full recognition as part of a comprehensive treaty.

Stress educational, scientific, and technological development

An educated community, which is an essential requirement for meaningful development, is either missing or very small in most Muslim societies and countries. Muslims have extremely low literacy rates, and they lag in science and technology. As a first step, they need to improve their literacy rate. The effort to create an educated society should start at the lowest level and extend to higher education. Meaningful incentives should be provided for achieving higher degrees, especially in engineering, science, and technology.

Muslims have the potential to be as successful as any other community, but they need education. Collectively, an educated community or group can achieve a lot, as exemplified by the Pakistani nuclear program which was developed by a few Muslim engineers and scientists in an underdeveloped country. They had the will and found the way against all odds to develop a nuclear bomb for ensuring Pakistan's survival.

Achieve economic independence

A study of the economies of Muslim countries reveals that the majority are weak financially and, hence, have limited economic and political independence. An economically dependent and financially strapped country has limited options and can rarely act independently even when its national interests are at stake. To achieve economic independence, Muslim countries must be prepared to make sacrifices they have not been willing to make in the past. They must be fiscally responsible, even though it might be beneficial in the short-term to act otherwise, or they will perpetuate too many long-term problems.

Many of the actions that leaders or governments take are in response to the demands of its citizens. If citizens cooperate, it is easier for the government to implement necessary measures. On the flip side, citizens can force the government to act responsibly and implement fiscally sound policies so that the economy is strengthened rather than weakened. Muslims need to understand these basic facts and do everything within their power to force their governments to act responsibly and, when required, cooperate with measures taken in the national interest.

Introduce social reform

Each Muslim country has unique social problems. They should be solved through the introduction of appropriate social reforms, which have been long overdue. Muslim societies should reflect the fairness and social equity that Islam enjoins—not the unfair systems they have implemented in violation of the Islamic principles they profess to follow.

Muslim societies need to respect and implement women's rights instead of just paying lip service. They should include women in education reform. Legal systems should be overhauled so that ordinary people can address grievances and hope to obtain justice, which is their fundamental right guaranteed by Islam.

The rights of workers should be respected. They are rarely honored in many Muslim societies. Bonded labor systems, where people are literally enslaved for life due to their own or inherited debt, should be banned. Land reforms need to be carried out in feudalistic societies so that those who work get the benefit of their labor.

Strive for unity

According to Islam, Muslims are expected to regard other Muslims as brothers and sisters in a united brotherhood. However, unity has been an elusive objective as Muslims have been divided since the time of the caliphs. There are problems, sometimes over trivial issues, between different sects and countries that periodically turn into serious intersect riots and result in bloodshed. Instead of focusing on differences, Muslims should unite and rise above petty considerations. They should respect and tolerate the views of others, Muslims and non-Muslims, as Islam enjoins. Muslims should unite in the achievement of common goals. If they are united, they will command greater respect and have greater clout than a disunited community can ever hope to achieve.

Shift from negative to positive objectives

The past few centuries have not been good for Muslims. This reality has influenced them negatively. Therefore, their objectives have tended to be more negative than positive. The negative urge to bring down or extract revenge is easier to implement than a goal of building something. Muslims should look forward, not back, and be constructive with positive objectives that will uplift them.

On the political front, Muslims should reconcile with estranged neighboring countries. They should rise above negative and painful events and, where applicable, prevent historical enmity from continuing. On the fiscal side, they should also have a positive approach and objectives. For example, a positive objective can be a goal to increase the country's revenues by 10 percent, which will help pay off an existing loan in a shorter period. A negative goal would be to obtain a $100 million loan to cover a deficit without aiming to raise revenues or cutting costs.

Become more responsible

Muslims should become more responsible and change their existing attitude of blaming others at both personal and collective levels. They should perform self-examinations frequently and accept their mistakes. They should stop blaming others for their problems. They need to be more open-minded and less prejudiced. Instead of jumping to conclusions, they should first attempt to evaluate the situation, circumstances, and motives thoroughly before blaming someone else. Performing self-analysis and acknowledging mistakes can never harm—only help.

Learn to help themselves

Muslims should not expect anyone to pull them out of their morass. They need to remind themselves of the Islamic belief that God does not help those who do not help themselves. Foreign aid, special treatment, protection, or sympathy will not help them in the long run. Muslims must change themselves—no one else can do this for them—to become as self-reliant as possible and solve their own problems.

Become politically active

The Muslim masses are usually not politically involved in their countries. Politicians have taken advantage of their lack of participation and, consequently, they have ended up being regulated and ruled by third-rate legislators and leaders. Also, in most Muslim countries and societies, professionals and high achievers do not become politicians. The political arena is left for underachievers and, in too many cases, men of questionable character for whom the legislature and government are passports to wealth. It is not surprising that leaders who come out of such systems are of low caliber and, in many cases, corrupt and shady. Every Muslim should become involved in his country's political process. Also, professionals and other highly educated individuals should enter the political arena to enhance its quality and performance.

Pick good leaders and make them accountable

Leaders are a reflection of the society they rule. Usually, with some exceptions, corrupt societies produce corrupt and incompetent leaders. Muslims must uplift their character where it is lacking and take on the responsibility of picking good leaders who reflect the character of the society that elects them.

Once in power, leaders should not be given a free hand. They should be made accountable for their actions and performance. Typically, when a corrupt ruler is removed, the new ruler does not prosecute the departing ruler. The reason for ignoring an ex-ruler's illegal activities is self-interest. The new ruler wants to continue a corrupt system which will protect him from prosecution when he ultimately leaves office. If prosecution does take place, the objective is often to ensure that the ex-ruler, a rival, will not return to power.

Silent majority should become vocal

Extremists are a very small percentage of the Muslim community. They do not reflect the thoughts, hopes, and aspirations of the average Muslim. Despite that, they have received disproportionate attention and headlines because the media, American as well as foreign, are too eager to report their vehement and inflammatory rhetoric. It is time for the Muslim majority to make themselves heard and end the tyranny of the extremists who have hijacked Islam.

Avoid self-righteous superiority syndrome

One of the identifying characteristics of Muslims in the modern world is self-righteousness. This is exemplified by an Arab Muslim who illegally parked his car and blocked a driveway in front of a house when he went to attend the Friday noon congregational prayer in California. When he came out of the mosque, the vexed homeowner, who had been unable to drive away due to his blocked driveway, confronted him. A heated exchange followed and the Muslim was abusive. When mosque management heard of the exchange, it asked the Muslim to apologize. The man refused saying, "I cannot apologize to a Christian!" Muslims should follow Islamic principles and judge issues based on merit and not according to the personalities, religions, or countries involved.

Communicate with non-Muslims

There are too many misunderstandings between Muslims and non-Muslims. Their removal should be a top priority for Muslims. They need to communicate with non-Muslims and try to remove misconceptions, misunderstandings, and false notions about Islam and Muslims. In the modern age, communication is a vital skill that Muslims sorely lack. They need to address this shortcoming and develop superior communication skills—at both the personal and community levels.

WHAT AMERICA AND THE WEST NEED TO DO

Address root causes of problems

Just like Muslims, the Western world needs to address the fundamental causes of its problems with the followers of Islam. It should make a serious effort to understand Islam and Muslims by engaging in a serious and constructive dialogue. The West, and especially Americans, must determine which mistakes were made and the causes of their problems with Muslims. Such issues should be addressed through active engagement and dialogue with Muslims at every level from personal to national.

Be a fair peace broker and guarantee Israel's security

America has the position and leverage to resolve the Arab-Israeli conflict if it is even-handed. It has not succeeded so far, despite serious attempts, because it has not acted as a neutral peace broker. America is still capable of resolving the conflict by meeting the second of the following three peace requirements:

- Arab responsibility: Israel must be granted full recognition by all its Arab neighbors
- American responsibility: America must guarantee Israel's security for 50 to 100 years
- Israeli responsibility: Israel must vacate all Arab lands captured since 1967

If Israel's security is guaranteed, it will not be able to use its small size as a pretext for retaining occupied territories. Arab neighbors will realize that Israel has been guaranteed its survival and act accordingly. It is recognized that there are many issues that will need to be worked out, including the right of return and free access to the holy sites in Jerusalem. However, all remaining issues will be far easier to settle once the three core issues (acceptance, security, and return of occupied lands) are resolved.

Be informed and sensitive

Western countries should be better informed about Islam and Muslims. The West, and Americans in particular, should do whatever it takes to understand Muslims and interact with them. For those who desire to be informed, there is no shortage of sources, especially on the Internet. There are thousands of mosques and Islamic centers in the Western world where useful information can be obtained. At such sites, Muslims can be observed first-hand as they go about their rituals, day-to-day religious and social activities, etc. These sites can also be the first point of contact for initiating a dialogue with members of the Islamic community.

Americans should be more sensitive and realize that there exists a world outside America with different beliefs and values. Americans should try to recognize, respect, and be sensitive to the differences that exist between the Islamic and Western civilizations. They should also avoid having a one-sided and patronizing attitude.

Plan for the long-term

American planning for the Middle East appears to be characterized and driven by the following factors:

- Demand for oil that must be fulfilled so the economy is not negatively impacted
- Desire for maintaining the status quo so oil supplies are not disrupted
- Ensuring that nothing is done to cause a fallout in the next election

The first item ensures that America will need to deal with the Middle East for the foreseeable future. The second item ensures that no step can be taken, even if it has the potential to provide long-term stability, if there is any chance of creating short-term supply issues. The third item ensures that no politically unpopular step can be taken, even if it leads to the long-term solution of the Middle East conflict, if it displeases the extremely powerful pro-Israeli lobby—which will happen if America becomes even-handed and tries to impose a just settlement.

In order to be successful, American policy must be fair and just. An even-handed American Middle East policy will lead to long-term stability in the region by providing justice to the people living there. Such a policy carries serious domestic risks and problems for any American leader who tries to support it. However, unless such a step is taken, or a breakthrough substitute is discovered that makes oil an expendable commodity, the Middle East problem will not go away. Unless America implements a fair policy and Middle East issues are resolved, it will remain in conflict with Muslims.

Match actions to words

Americans must practice what they preach. They cannot be selective in the application of the principles they honor. Americans should treat all violators of human rights in the same way. A friendly country that commits a crime must be treated the same as a rogue state. If democracy is a valued principle, then dictators in friendly and unfriendly countries should be treated or penalized equally. If a friendly country is guilty of state-sponsored terrorism, it should be treated no differently than an unfriendly state committing the same crime. Similarly, calls for the restoration of human rights should be addressed to all violators and not just unfriendly nations.

Be unbiased and fair

While there are many issues between Muslims and the Western world, only a few can be classified as serious and very difficult to solve. The major problem that has created Muslim animosity against the West, and especially against America, is the Palestinian issue. It is the core issue that drives everything else in the Middle East. While Europeans are fairer in their approach, due to their proximity and greater dependence on imported oil, Americans need to go a long way before they can be considered fair. Until Americans are perceived to be even-handed in the Middle East and other places where Muslim interests are involved, hatred for America will not dissipate.

Do not paint all with the same brush

Muslims are very diverse politically, culturally, and socially. They are spread out all over the world and should not be stereotyped. One of the most common mistakes non-Muslims make is to confuse Muslims and

Arabs. Only about 22 percent of Muslims are Arabs. The result of this confusion is that some of the Arab and Palestinian fallout has negatively impacted non-Arab Muslims. Care should be taken to ensure that each group is judged by its actions and deeds unless there is a clear trend that can be related to all Muslims.

Engage Muslims

Living in silos is the perfect way to create misunderstandings between any two groups. To avoid such a situation, non-Muslims should make a serious effort to communicate with Muslims. Interaction will help eradicate stereotypes and misconceptions. It will also help build a good relationship based on many shared values and beliefs. Interaction will also show that in day-to-day life, Muslims and non-Muslims face the same issues, problems, and challenges. Interfaith meetings and exchanges should be encouraged. Visiting mosques and the homes of Muslims will remove many barriers and misconceptions. Other ways to engage Muslims should be fully explored and utilized.

Build on common values

There is no dearth of common values between Muslims and the Western world, which is predominantly Christian and Jewish, faiths that Islam respects. Belief in God is a basic Islamic and Judeo-Christian principle. Muslims, Christians, and Jews share high moral values, family values, business and ethical values, respect for human rights, etc. These and other common values should be identified and built upon to create mutual understanding and respect.

WHAT AMERICAN MUSLIMS NEED TO DO

Assume world leadership

Muslims in America are diverse and highly educated. Excluding Black Muslims, the majority of Muslims are either first- or second-generation immigrants from the Middle East, Far East, or Africa. They have been exposed to and understand the Muslim thought process and psychology. These Muslims also understand the West, which puts them in a unique position to become the bridge between the West and Islam. American Muslims should lead the way for world Muslims, which is only possible if they act in a united way. American Muslims can lead only if they show Muslims in the rest of the world their successes in a modern society and in building a model Muslim community.

Leave baggage behind

Many immigrant American Muslim leaders bring a lot of baggage from their countries of origin. Some reflect non-democratic methods of operating institutions, the way other sects or women are treated, etc. These leaders tend to take actions and positions detrimental to their local Muslim community. Frequently, their actions become the basis for infighting and splits that project a negative image. A common cause for splits is the tendency of some Muslim community leaders to follow the Saudis, whom they consider to be on the spiritual high ground, even though the majority do not share their view. Muslims in America should think and act independently without being manipulated by, or being beholden to, external governments and organizations.

Focus on the bigger picture

Many American Muslims have lost sight of the big picture and, instead, focus on trivial issues that have divided their community and prevented them from moving forward. These include issues such as control of mosques, election of officers, deciding which days the Eid festivals should be celebrated, whether women should be allowed on a mosque's governing board, Friday sermon language (English or Arabic), whether one or two persons should deliver the Friday sermon, etc.

For Muslims, bigger issues have typically taken the back stage. Issues such as how to marginalize extremists, national issues that have the potential to impact the viability of Muslims as a community, how to keep youth interested in Islam, and how to bring non-practicing Muslims into the fold should be focused upon rather than trivial issues that split the community and cause important issues to be ignored.

Put own house in order

The image of American Muslims in America is mixed. At work, they command respect and are recognized as dedicated workers. However, they have also created negative opinions in neighborhoods across the country. Many mosques have become neighborhood problems due to widespread illegal parking, especially at the Friday afternoon prayer time and during evenings in the fasting month of Ramadan. If mosque leaders cannot manage basic tasks such as ensuring proper parking, starting prayers on time, running democratic administrations, and letting women run for office, it is a poor reflection on their capability to lead. Unless they learn to practice what they preach, such as Islamic consideration for neighbors, a negative image will continue to be projected about Islam. It is imperative that Muslims develop the respect and trust of Americans through personal actions and the way they run their institutions.

Avoid double standards

Orthodox Muslims throughout the world insist that their women wear hejab, a headscarf, which they believe is an Islamic requirement. However, despite being religious, many mistreat their women, mentally and physically, and deny them the basic rights Islam guarantees. In America and the Western countries also, many orthodox Muslim men insist that their women wear hejab and that their daughters be educated at home. However, these same men have no hesitation in working with women who wear revealing clothes at work. If they had the courage of their convictions, they would walk off their jobs and trust God to provide them with an income, a belief that true Muslims are expected to have. Such people have weak beliefs or double standards. The application of double standards, which is a universal problem, extends to many areas. Muslims everywhere should make a determined effort to identify and rectify questionable or unfair practices.

Lead by example and marginalize extremists

Muslims in America have to act as ambassadors of Islam. The example they set becomes the basis by which Americans relate Islam to Muslims. They must be proactive and open dialogues with non-Muslims. They must become the catalyst for starting communication with members of other communities and correcting misunderstandings.

Muslims in America have a difficult task in raising their children in a society where it is easy to deviate from Islam. They must use a middle-of-the-road approach, which Islam enjoins, that strikes a balance between religion and the worldly life. They also have a duty to ensure that extremist elements within the community are marginalized through their own active participation in community affairs. They need to speak up as forcefully in denouncing terrorism and tyranny of the extremists just like many non-Muslim Americans, led by President Bush, spoke up on behalf of Muslims and Islam. They need to support

Muslim leaders like Hamza Yusuf, who spoke up fearlessly in support of his beliefs and rejection of terrorism.

Plan for the long-term

There is widespread stereotyping of Muslims in America. Negative press far outweighs positive reports and stories. Talk show hosts are having a field day bashing Muslims and Islam. Muslims are not able to communicate or respond effectively and are depressed by the barrage of one-sided news. They need to realize that their history in America is very short. It takes time to organize and become effective. A cursory study of Jewish history reveals that for a long time they were discriminated against and stereotyped in America. At this time also, Jews face discrimination in many areas of the country. Initially, they were not organized to face their unique challenges. Over time, they have created superior communication and organizational capabilities that can be quickly mobilized to address any issue. Muslims must have long-term objectives and work diligently to achieve them.

Be involved in the political process

American Muslims should become involved in politics at the grass-roots level. A community as large as the Muslims, numbering in the millions, needs to become mainstream and be represented in local government, state legislatures, and Congress. Unless they have their own representatives, Muslims can never hope to be heard where it counts. Even if they cannot elect Muslim representatives at this time, they have the strength to become swing vote blocks in many districts. A difference of even a few individual votes, or blocks of votes, can make a significant difference, as was demonstrated in the Florida vote in the 2000 presidential election. With their ability to swing election results, legislators will be forced to listen and address Muslim issues. However, Muslims first need to become part of the election process in a meaningful way.

Master communication techniques

One of the most important tools in the modern world is communication. In the past, Muslims did not realize the importance of this tool or use it in an organized manner. They have started to address that shortcoming and have organized at least one very effective group—Council for American and Islamic Relations (CAIR). Over the past few years, CAIR has rebutted many incorrect news stories and perceptions about Muslims. It has also managed to pressure many American companies to apologize or reverse corporate actions viewed as anti-Muslim.

Over time, organizations such as CAIR will prove beneficial in projecting the correct image of Muslims and rebutting incorrect information. However, to be even more effective, communications need to be extended beyond issuing rebuttals and statements. Serious efforts should be made proactively to communicate with power centers, groups, and individuals throughout the country.

A challenge for Muslims is to prevent their communications and public relations organizations, such as CAIR, from deviating from their stated purpose and objectives or allowing leadership to pass to those with a different and undesirable agenda.

Stress common values

There are many common religious, moral, and family values shared by Muslims, Christians, and Jews. Muslims believe in free enterprise and entrepreneurship, ethics in business, democracy, and other values that are the foundations of Western societies. Common values should be stressed by American Muslims and used as the basis for dialogues and promoting better understanding for their religion.

Develop mirror image of society professionals

At this time, most Muslims in America want their offspring to focus on a few professions such as medicine, engineering, and computer science.

They should also stress other equally important fields such as journalism, law, communications, marketing, etc. The Muslim community should include professionals from all fields who can extend the reach of Muslims to all sections of society. Such professionals will enable it to communicate with, and better understand, the people of the country they live in.

Appreciate what America has provided

There are some Muslims who, despite living in America, love to bash it. They participate in the American Dream and enjoy its benefits, including economic and financial opportunities, lack of discrimination, personal freedom, freedom of speech, and religious freedom. Despite enjoying these benefits, they find fault with everything American. Such people, who are performing a great disservice to Muslims, should compare what they left behind in their former countries with what they are experiencing now. If America is not better, or the country they came from is faultless, they should go back. America has its faults, but it is the responsibility of those living here, including Muslims, to rectify them. For that, a democratic process exists and Muslims can participate in it just like other citizens.

Reach out for a better future

The name of Islam was used to justify a criminal act by Osama bin Laden and the al-Qaeda organization. Similarly, there are powerful elements in America which, to serve their own purposes and agendas, have been smearing Islam and Muslims. 9-11 has been a godsend for people who have used the event to their advantage by employing scare tactics and spreading false information about Islam and its followers, primarily by associating terrorist actions with Islam.

9-11 caused a paradigm shift. It made Americans acutely aware that something was seriously wrong and that they were hated. They have since been conducting their own investigations, researching on the Internet, visiting mosques, meeting local Islamic organizations, talking to Muslim colleagues at work, studying the Koran, and most importantly asking themselves a lot of questions about why the 9-11 tragedy occurred. Many have been surprised by what they discovered about Islam and Muslims, the prevalence of false notions about Islam, Islamic beliefs shared by Christians and Jews, the extent to which news reaching them had been filtered, etc. Consequently, it has led many to rethink and reevaluate their views about Islam and Muslims.

Muslims were shocked by what happened on 9-11. They too have started to seriously analyze the 9-11 act and its implications, the current conditions of Muslims and how they developed, why they are being viewed as terrorists, and how a terrorist organization hijacked Islam.

The combination of change and reevaluation among Muslims and Americans is very positive. It provides hope that the two groups will be able to build on common ground and start a new chapter with foundations of respect, tolerance, justice, and mutual understanding. There have been mistakes on both sides. If both sides look forward and learn from the past, there can be high expectations for a better, peaceful, and prosperous future for everyone.

APPENDIX
CHRONOLOGY OF HISTORICAL EVENTS

570	Prophet Muhammad is born
610	Muhammad receives first revelation
622	Muhammad flees to Medina from Mecca; start of Islamic State and Society
630	Conquest of Mecca
632	Muhammad dies
632–661	Rule of four Caliphs
661–750	Ummayyad Dynasty
710	Muslims forces land in Spain
732	Battle of Tours in France
750–1258	Abbassid Dynasty
750–950	Golden Age of Islam
756	Ummayyad Dynasty restarts in Spain
813–833	Reign of al-Mamun Abbassid
909–1171	Fatimid Dynasty in Egypt
1055-1243	Rule of the Seljuks
1095	First Crusade
1099	Crusaders take Jerusalem
1171	Salahuddin ends Fatimid Dynasty in Egypt and founds the Ayyubid Dynasty

1187	Salahuddin retakes Jerusalem
1258	Mongol invaders under Halagu Khan attack Baghdad and execute the Abbassid Caliph
1299–1922	Ottoman Empire
1453	Turkish Ottomans conquer Constantinople and rename it Istanbul
1492	Christians under Isabella capture Granada—last Muslim kingdom in Spain
1501–1722	Safavid Empire in Persia
1526	Mughal Empire established in India
1529	First Ottoman siege of Vienna
1683	Second Ottoman siege of Vienna
1830	France occupies Algeria
1857	Last Mughal ruler in India deposed by British
1882	Egypt is occupied by Britain
1902	Saud Dynasty established in Arabia
1917	Balfour Declaration
1922	Turkish Sultanate abolished; Egypt becomes nominally independent from Britain
1924	Caliphate abolished in Turkey
1946	Jordan, Lebanon and Syria became independent
1947	India freed by British and partitioned into India and Pakistan
1948	Israel created
1949	Indonesia becomes independent
1953	Mossadegh overthrown in Iran
1956	Second Arab-Israeli war; Suez Canal crisis

1967	Six-day Arab-Israeli war
1973	Fourth Arab-Israeli war; Arab oil embargo
1979	Iranian Revolution; Bhutto is hanged in Pakistan
1980-1988	Iran-Iraq war
1989	Armed revolt starts against Indian occupation in Kashmir; breakup of Soviet Union
1979–1989	Afghanistan war following Soviet invasion
1982	Israeli invasion of Lebanon
1990	Iraq invades Kuwait
1998	Pakistan conducts nuclear tests
2001	9-11 terrorist attack on America
2002	Israel invades West Bank

INDEX

20th century, 17, 21, 27, 39, 49, 65, 72, 89
21st century, 19
9-11, 46-47, 53, 56-58, 60, 70-71, 74-75, 85, 94, 131-132, 135
Abbassid, 6, 11-12, 133-134
Abbassids, 5-6, 12-13
Abd al-Wahhab, 27
abolished, 15, 27, 134
abortion, 45, 66, 110, 112
Abraham, 2
acceptance, 101, 122
Adam, 1-2
Aden, 15
Afghanistan, 5, 34-35, 46-48, 53, 55-56, 58, 71-72, 93-95, 107, 113, 135
Afghans, 14, 34-35, 66
Africa, 2, 5-6, 8, 11-12, 17, 27-28, 126
African slaves, 21
African-Americans, 21-22
aggressor, 36
agriculture, 6
al-Aqsa, 32, 82, 89
al-Assad, Hafez, 48, 65
al-Biruni, 9
algebra, 6, 9
Algeciras conference, 15
al-Hasan, 9
Ali ibn Abu Talib, 4
Ali, Muhammad, 76
al-Khawarizmi, 9
alliances, 13
al-Mamun, 7, 11, 133
al-Qaeda, 55-56, 72, 131
al-Rashid, Harun, 11
al-Razi, 10
altitude, 6
al-Zahrawi, Khalaf Abul-Qasim, 10
al-Zawahri, Ayman, 28
ambassadors, 128
America, 21-23, 31-32, 34, 37, 39, 41-42, 44-50, 52-54, 56, 58-73, 75-76, 78, 80, 83, 85, 87-88, 90, 96, 98, 100, 102, 104, 112, 116, 121-124, 126-131, 135
American and Western way of life, 45, 67
American Dream, 131

American Muslims, 22-23, 57, 96, 126-127, 129-130
American troops, 38, 45, 56, 66-67, 114
Amnesty International, 31, 41-42
anatomy, 6, 9
Anglo-Iranian Oil Company, 32
annual rate, 19
apathetic, 87
Arab royal families, 28
Arab sheikhdoms, 15
Arab-dominated, 5
Arabia, 1-2, 15, 17, 29, 36-39, 45, 56, 66-67, 83, 85, 94, 114, 134, 138
Arabian Peninsula, 3-4, 12
Arabic numerals, 6
Arab-Israeli war, 33-34, 134-135
Arabs, 8, 12, 16-17, 19-21, 32-34, 45, 50, 60-62, 68-69, 71, 90, 111, 116, 125
Arafat, Yasser, 63
Argentina, 16
arms supplies, 36
arts, 6
Asia Minor, 12, 14
assassination, 4
astrolabe, 6, 9
astronomy, 6, 8-9
Ataturk, Mustafa Kemal, 27
Atlantic, 5
Babar, 14
Babri mosque, 30, 85
baggage, 126
Baghdad, 5-7, 12-13, 134

Bakr, Abu, 4
Balfour Declaration, 16, 77, 134
Bangladesh, 5, 17, 19
Bank of Credit and Commerce, 38
banned organizations, 72
Banu Musa, 9
Basque ETA, 111
Battle of Tours, 3, 5, 133
BCCI, 38
Begin, Menachem, 44
beholden, 126
Belgium, 43, 50
benchmark, 26
Berbers, 13
Bhutto, 39-40, 48, 80, 84, 92, 135
bin Laden, Osama, 28, 56, 87, 94, 100, 131
Black Muslim movement, 21-22, 76
blatant discrimination, 30
blood circulation, 6
bloody, 17, 35, 47, 84, 95
Bonaparte, Napoleon, 15
books, 7, 9, 45, 49, 70-71, 138
borders, 5
born-again Christians, 66
Bosnia, 15, 19, 35-36, 54-55, 75-76, 114
breakup of the Soviet Union, 35
bridges, 59, 98
British crown, 15
British government, 32
brotherhood, 8, 20, 28, 118
brothers, 20, 118
brutal, 17, 47, 91, 93

Buchanan, Pat, 68
budget deficit, 37
Bukhara, 5
Burma, 14
burning, 36, 109
burqa, 65-66
Bush, 43, 75, 97, 100, 128
business interests, 31-32, 64
Byzantine Empire, 4, 14
CAIR, 130
caliph, 3-6, 27, 101, 134
caliphate, 4, 6, 12, 15, 27, 134
canal, 33-34, 41, 78, 134
captured, 5-6, 13-14, 26, 29, 35, 122
captured territories, 13
Catholics, 61, 70, 111
cease-fire, 30-31, 34
center of learning, 6
CENTO, 31, 46
Central Asia, 2, 5, 12-13, 35
character, 18, 90, 119-120
characteristics, 18, 20, 52, 86, 121
chemistry, 6
China, 3, 5, 13, 31-32, 46
Christian kingdoms, 13
Christianity, 18-19, 22, 68, 100, 107, 112
Christians, 3, 5, 26, 66-68, 82, 101, 103-104, 107, 111-112, 125, 130, 132, 134
CIA, 33
citizens, 49, 52-53, 72, 94, 107, 110, 117, 131
civil war, 35, 37, 47, 70, 84, 93-94

coalition, 35-36, 48, 66, 83
Cold War, 31, 33, 64-65, 72
college graduates, 23
colonial empires, 27
colonial expansion, 16
colonial subjugation, 15-16
colonized, 14
Commission of Inquiry, 43
common faith, 20
common values, 66, 125, 130
communication, 121, 128-130
communist government, 34
communists, 34, 72, 94
community affairs, 128
community centers, 23
compulsion in religion, 81, 101-102
conflict, 4, 16, 35, 41, 50, 55, 64, 68, 75, 108, 113, 116, 122-124
Congress, 61-62, 73, 129
conquering forces, 3
consolidate, 3, 31
consortium, 33
conspiracy, 29, 53, 83
Constantinople, 14, 134
continents, 20
contributed, 7-8, 16, 88, 93
contributions, 6-7, 9
control, 3, 5, 11-12, 17, 27, 29, 32, 34, 42, 53, 58, 63, 77, 80, 85, 127
conventional war, 40
converted, 5, 8, 22, 76, 97, 102-104
converts, 21

core issue, 124
corruption, 52, 63, 89, 92-93, 113
Council for American and Islamic Relations, 130
counterweight, 48
coup, 33, 39, 93
credit markets, 37
crimes against humanity, 43, 50
crises, 21, 37, 59, 74, 78, 114
cross-migration, 17
Crusades, 5, 12, 26, 53, 107
cultural center, 6
cultural diversity, 20
customs, 18, 20
damage, 12, 95
Dark Ages, 8
deaths in custody, 31
decentralization, 6
decline, 11, 13, 26-27, 52, 79, 89
defeat, 5, 27, 29, 34, 36, 68
defector, 21
defense of Islam, 35, 105, 107
defiance, 43
delineated, 28
demarcation, 29
democracies, 20
democracy, 18, 64-65, 79, 85, 90, 93, 97, 113, 124, 130
demolished, 30
demonstrators, 69
deposed, 14, 27, 134
Desert Storm, 38
despots, 44, 64-65, 89-90
destruction, 13, 35, 41-43, 51, 57, 89, 94, 99, 101-103, 109
deterrent, 40
devastated, 13, 83
development, 6-9, 27, 29, 46, 76, 87, 116
diagnosis, 115
dialogue, 122-123
dictators, 44, 64-65, 89-90, 124
disappearances, 31
dishonest, 52
disintegrated, 12-13
dissection, 6
distributed, 5
distribution, 7, 19, 23, 91, 113
distribution of Muslims, 19
disunited, 21, 118
diversity, 20
divide-and-rule policy, 50-51
division, 12, 15
divorce, 92
doctors, 23
domestic affairs, 73
domestic news, 71, 74
double standards, 47, 128
driven out, 15, 76
drugs, 6, 92
due process, 41, 50
dynasties, 11, 14, 101-103
economic condition, 26
economic development, 29, 116

economically, 32, 34, 51, 53, 77, 79, 89, 94, 96, 117
education, 7, 16, 18, 22, 29, 66, 78-79, 84, 95, 112-113, 116-117
Egypt, 4, 6, 12-13, 15, 17, 19, 28, 33-34, 36, 65, 71, 77-78, 91, 133-134
elections, 47-48, 62, 84, 90, 92-93
embargo, 33-34, 36, 39, 49, 61-62, 91, 135
emigrate, 14, 21
empires, 4, 11, 27
enemies, 17, 82
engagement principles, 75
engineers, 23, 40, 117
escaped, 6
establishment, 3, 6-7, 16, 25, 27
ethnic cleansing, 36, 54, 75-76
ethnic diversity, 20
ethnic divisions, 20
ethnic groups, 5, 20, 50
European Christians, 5
European Muslims, 21
executed, 6, 33, 77, 84
executions, 31, 36
exiled, 14
expansion, 3, 6, 16, 33, 38, 42, 102
expansionist power, 61
expeditions, 5, 26, 102
exploiting, 81
exporting, 28, 55, 95
extended, 2, 4-5, 12-13, 130
external threats, 13
extrajudicial executions, 31
extremist schools, 28
fair-minded, 60
fall of communism, 35
fall of Spain, 13
Fatimid dynasty, 12, 133
Fatimids, 6, 12
Feisal, 39, 94
figurehead leader, 27
filtered, 132
financially strapped, 117
firepower, 27
flourishing, 6
foot soldiers, 55
forced conversions, 99, 102-104, 106
foreign issues, 65, 73
foreign policy, 38, 56, 61, 64, 68-69, 73
Fourth Geneva Convention, 42
France, 3, 5, 15-17, 19, 28, 91, 133-134
friday, 96-97, 121, 127
fringe groups, 49
frustration, 34
fundamental and human rights, 18, 48
future, 7, 16, 32, 48, 50, 59, 87, 97, 115, 123, 131-132, 138
gasoline, 34, 61
gay rights, 45
Gaza Strip, 32-33
geography, 9
Germany, 15-16, 19
Ghazni, Mahmud, 14
ghetto-like conditions, 32
Gibraltar, 5

Golan Heights, 33
Golden Age of Islam, 6, 11, 40, 101, 103, 133
governor, 4, 77
Granada, 14, 134
Guardian of Islam, 84
guerrilla campaign, 34
Gujarat, 30, 86
Gulf War, 35, 37-38, 45, 48, 65, 67, 83
Gurdaspur, 77
Habbash, George, 82
Halabja, 47
Hama, 48, 91, 109
Hamas, 50, 63, 81, 83
harming civilians, 105
hate, 42, 45, 51, 53-54, 57, 67-68, 76, 83
heavenly bodies, 6
heinous crimes, 36
hejab, 128
helplessness, 34
Herzl, Theodor, 16
Hezbollah, 36
hijackers, 57, 85
Hindu-Muslim riots, 17
Hindus, 17, 29-30, 80-82
Hitler, 16, 100
holy city, 67
Holy Land, 5, 67
House of Representatives, 62
human rights, 31
Human Rights Watch, 31, 43, 86
humanitarian, 37, 42, 109

humiliation, 34, 83
Hungary, 15
Hussein, Saddam, 44, 47, 48, 49, 65, 83, 90, 100, 109
Iberian Peninsula, 5
ibn Affan, Uthman, 4
ibn al-Haytham, 10
ibn al-Saud, Muhammad, 27
ibn Batuta, 9
ibn Khaldun, 9
ibn Muhammad, Marwan, 5
ibn Qurra, Thabit, 9
ibn Sina, 9-10
identity, 21
ideology, 27, 47, 55
Ikhwan al-Muslimeen, 28
illiterate, 30, 40
immigrants, 21-22, 97, 126
implement, 18, 42, 48, 115, 117-118
implementation of UN resolutions, 31
implications, 4, 48, 132
incited, 16
incompetent, 89-90, 93, 120
independence, 16-17, 28-29, 35-36, 53, 69, 71, 82, 93, 117
independent, 6, 28-29, 39, 47, 68, 77, 93, 97, 134
India, 5, 13-15, 17, 19, 29-31, 40, 46, 48-51, 67, 77, 80, 85, 101, 103, 111, 134
Indian army, 31, 109
Indian subcontinent, 5, 14, 19, 103

Indonesia, 5, 17, 19, 28, 65, 93, 102-104, 134
ineffectual, 14, 36
influence, 4-5, 7-8, 12, 16, 50, 52, 61-62, 77, 97, 115
influence of Islam, 8
inheritance, 4, 56
innocent civilians, 56-57
Inquisition, 14
instrument, 6
interfaith meetings, 125
internal conflicts, 12
internal dissension, 13
internal issues, 4
international law, 43, 50
interrogation, 42
intolerant religion, 81, 102
invasion, 14-15, 35, 43, 135
invented, 9
IRA, 70, 87, 108, 111
Iran, 4-6, 13-14, 32-33, 36, 44, 48, 54, 65, 72, 77-78, 83, 91, 95, 134
Iranians, 33, 48, 83
Iran-Iraq war, 90, 95, 135
Iraq, 4, 6, 12-13, 15-17, 28-29, 31, 35, 48-50, 65, 72, 77, 83, 114, 135
Irgun Zvai Leumi, 111
Irish Republican Army, 70
Isabella, 14, 101, 134
Islam, 1-8, 11-13, 18-22, 25-26, 35, 40, 52, 55-58, 66-68, 70, 74-82, 84, 86-89, 91-95, 97-114, 117-118, 120-122, 125-129, 131-133
Islamic bomb, 51
Islamic civilization, 6-9, 11, 25-26
Islamic country, 29, 80, 92
Islamic Empire, 2-6, 11-12, 14, 103
Islamic force, 5
Islamic heartland, 13
Islamic history, 55
Islamic Jehad, 28, 50, 81
Islamic law, 20, 94-95
Islamic practice, 4
Islamic Salvation Front, 47, 93
Islamic society, 2-3, 25, 28
Israel, 17, 32-33, 36, 41-42, 47-48, 50-51, 53, 58, 60-63, 68, 82-83, 109, 111-112, 116, 122, 134-135
Istanbul, 14, 134
Italy, 15, 33
jehad, 28, 35, 50, 55, 71, 81, 88, 99, 105-108, 113
Jenin, 42, 109
Jerusalem, 3-4, 12, 26, 32-33, 83, 89, 101, 103, 111, 122, 133-134
Jesus, 2
Jewish immigration, 16
Jewish senators, 61-62
Jewish state, 16-17, 81
Jews, 3, 26, 32, 46, 54, 60-62, 67, 76, 81, 97, 101, 103, 125, 129-130, 132

justice, 4, 18, 39, 47, 54-55, 92, 94-95, 105, 113, 118, 124, 132
Kaaba, 94
Kahan Israeli Commission of Inquiry, 43
Kashmir, 30-31, 48-49, 55, 77, 81-82, 85, 103, 109-110, 114, 135
Kazakhstan, 12, 35
Khan, Genghis, 13-14
Khan, Halagu, 13
Khayyam, Umar, 9
Khomeni, 91, 95
Khorasan, 5
killed, 4, 17, 30-31, 43, 48, 55, 57, 83, 85, 92-94, 103, 107, 110
killing, 13, 37, 43, 57, 61, 81, 85, 108-109, 111
kingdoms, 13
Kissinger, 39
KKK, 87, 109
knowledge, 6-8, 18, 28, 55, 60, 65-66, 73-74, 78, 84, 102
Koran, 57, 78-79, 100-102, 108, 132
Koresh, David, 87, 100
Kosovo, 54, 76, 114
Kyrgystan, 12
leaders, 3, 16, 18, 29-30, 39, 44, 50, 55, 58, 62-63, 65, 69, 72, 75-76, 81-82, 86-87, 89-92, 94, 96-98, 100, 117, 119-120, 126-127, 129
leadership, 4, 20, 39, 43, 51, 58, 81, 83, 86-87, 89-90, 94-97, 113, 126, 130

Lebanon, 16-17, 28-29, 36-37, 43, 134-135
legacy, 13, 51
libraries, 7-9, 13
Libya, 15, 17, 28, 91, 102
lip service, 18, 21, 117
literacy, 78-79, 116
literature, 6
living conditions, 7
local practice, 20
Lockerbie, 91, 100
long-term threat, 32
machinations, 29
madrassas, 28, 84, 95
mainstream Islam, 21, 76
Malaysia, 5, 17, 28
Malcolm X, 21, 76
Mamluks, 13
Man of Peace, 43
manipulation, 90
marginalize extremists, 127-128
Marine barracks, 37
martyr, 110
mass executions, 36
mass illiteracy, 18
massacred, 26, 48, 91
mathematics, 6-9
meaningful protest, 35
measuring, 6
Mecca, 3, 20, 32, 67, 94, 133
media, 45, 51, 62-63, 68-71, 85-88, 100, 106-107, 120

medicine, 6-9, 86, 130
Medina, 3-4, 20, 32, 67, 133
MI6, 33
Middle East, 2, 12, 15, 17, 19, 22, 28, 37, 39, 43, 47-48, 53-54, 58, 60-61, 64, 68, 74-75, 111-112, 123-124, 126
migrated, 3, 29-30
migration, 17, 30
military, 3, 5, 20, 28, 30-31, 33-34, 38, 42, 45-46, 48, 64-65, 67, 72, 75-76, 84, 90, 92
military bases, 45, 67
military dictatorships, 20
military intervention, 33
military support, 34, 67
militiamen, 43
misinformation, 69, 88
misinterpretation, 88
mistakes, 52, 59, 72-73, 97, 119, 122, 125, 132
Mizos, 111
mobilizing, 81-82
moderation, 113
modernize, 27
monarchies, 20
Mongols, 6, 8, 12-13, 20, 102
Moses, 2
mosques, 23, 96-97, 123, 125, 127, 131
Mossadegh, 32-33, 64-65, 77-78, 134
Mountbatten, 77
movements, 6, 27-28, 82, 108
Muawiyah, 4, 6

Muawiyah, Abd al-Rahman ibn, 6
Mubarak, Hosni, 65, 91
Mughal Empire, 14, 134
Muhammad, 2-5, 8, 25, 27, 76, 78, 94-95, 101, 108, 133
mujahideen, 35, 55, 71-72, 94
mullah, xvii
multinational domain, 5
murdered, 4, 39, 92, 111
Muslim Brotherhood, 28
Muslim dynasties, 11, 14, 101, 103
Muslim history, 16
Muslim rulers, 3, 80, 107
Nagas, 111
naked aggression, 83
national boundaries, 29
national home, 16
nationalists, 55
nationalization, 32
Native Americans, 42
negative press, 82, 129
neighbors, 14, 17, 33, 50, 61, 81, 83, 90, 107, 122, 127
New York Times, 43
newspapers, 45, 70-71, 74
Nigeria, 19, 28
nominally, 12, 28, 134
non-Arabs, 21
non-believers, 100
non-practicing Muslims, 127
North Africa, 2, 5-6, 11-12
nuclear power, 39

objectives, 26-27, 29, 57, 64, 66, 82, 88, 112-113, 118-119, 129-130
observatory, 6
occupation forces, 36, 49, 60, 71, 108
occupying power, 93, 108
ocean navigation, 9
official religion, 13, 92
oil embargo, 34, 39, 61-62, 135
oil industry, 32, 77-78
oil resources, 29, 32, 77, 91
oil-rich, 29, 34, 37, 91
OPEC, 61
Operation Ajax, 33
oppressed countries, 44
Organization of Islamic Conference (OIC), 89-90
Osman, 14
Ottoman Empire, 14-16, 26-29, 134
Ottomans, 14-15, 134
overthrow, 28, 32-33, 77-78
Oxus, 5
Pakistan, 5, 17, 19, 28-31, 36, 39-40, 46, 50, 64-65, 69, 77, 80, 84, 92, 117, 134-135
Palestine, 6, 12, 16-17, 29, 32, 41-42, 54-55, 60, 62-63, 77, 81-82, 109-111, 114
Palestine Liberation Organization, 63, 82
Panipat, 14
paper, 6-7, 16
paramilitary personnel, 31
parliamentary, 20, 92
partition, 16, 17, 29, 30, 77, 134

patronized, 23, 28, 92
patronizing, 123
peace broker, 122
peaceful movement, 17
peak, 7-8, 11, 15-16
Pentagon, 56
performance, 40, 101, 120, 138
permanent peace, 17
perpetrator, 42
persecute, 16
Persia, 4, 14, 134
Persian Gulf, 15, 96
personal attributes, 52
personal characteristics, 18
personal struggle, 106
Phalange Christian militia, 42
Philippines, 5
philosophy, 6
physics, 9
pillaging, 36
PLO, 50, 63
pogroms, 30
Poland, 15
police, 30, 91
political capital, 115
political center, 5
political diversity, 20
political independence, 53, 117
political leaders, 18, 96
political payoffs, 28
political process, 120, 129
political stability, 47

political unity, 21
Pope, 26, 87
Popular Front for the Liberation of Palestine (PFLP), 82
population, 16-19, 21-22, 31, 41, 45, 48-49, 61-62, 66, 69, 76, 90-91, 96, 101, 103
positions, 6, 18, 90, 95, 126
power, 3-6, 12, 14-15, 27, 33-34, 39-40, 42, 44, 47-48, 53, 58, 61, 67, 80, 84, 91, 93-94, 106-108, 117, 120, 130
power centers, 130
power struggles, 12
practices, 18, 20, 66, 90, 112, 128
practicing Muslims, 54-55
prejudiced, 54, 119
president, 37, 43, 60, 73, 75, 92, 97, 100, 128
presidential election, 73, 129
pretext, 122
price of oil, 34
pricing power, 34
principles of Islam, 18
prioritization, 79, 115-116
professionals, 23, 119-120, 130-131
pro-Israeli lobby, 123
prophet, 1-2, 78, 94-95, 108, 133
provinces, 6, 11
proxy, 34, 46
public opinion polls, 61, 75
racial groups, 8
raid, 5

Ramadan, 127
rapes, 31
Razi, 9
rebellion, 5, 31
recognize, 116, 123
recognized, 11, 13, 15, 100, 104, 116, 122, 127
recruits, 54-56
reform, 27, 117
refugees, 17, 32, 60
regions, 3, 5, 54, 81
relatives, 4, 22
religious, 3-4, 7, 18, 20, 27-28, 32, 35, 39, 45, 54-56, 58, 62-63, 66, 69-70, 80-84, 86-87, 89, 92-97, 100, 104, 112-113, 123, 128, 130-131
religious backgrounds, 7
religious beliefs, 28, 104
religious extremism, 28
religious extremists, 28, 69, 80-81
religious fundamentalists, 80, 84, 112
religious organizations, 28, 63
religious revival, 27
Religious Right, 66
religious zealots, 28, 84, 100
Renaissance, 7-8
repression, 47
resentment, 45, 56
resistance, 2-3, 13, 36, 54-55, 63, 81-83
resources, 29, 32, 40, 77, 91, 116
respect, 65, 90, 100, 113, 117-118, 123, 125, 127, 132

restarted, 6
resurgence, 35, 114
revolt, 14, 16-17, 29, 35, 135
right of self-determination, 31, 48
riots, 17, 30, 84-85, 118
rival, 4, 120
role models, 86
root cause, 52, 63, 67-68, 83
rout, 36
ruling class, 49
Russia, 5, 13, 35, 104
Russians, 8, 20, 33, 109
Sabra, 42-43
sacrilege, 45, 67
Safavid Empire, 14, 134
Salahuddin, 12, 26, 103, 133-134
Samarkand, 5
Saudi Arabia, 17, 29, 36-39, 45, 56, 66-67, 83, 85, 94, 114, 138
Saudi dynasty, 27
Saudi export, 85
Saudi royal family, 27, 39, 84, 94
SAVAK, 91
scandals, 74
science, 6-8, 116, 130, 138
scientific manuscripts, 7
scientists, 8-9, 13, 23, 40, 117
SEATO, 31, 46
secular, 4, 15, 27-28, 52, 63, 69-70, 78, 81-82, 84, 86, 95-96, 113
secular state, 15, 27
security, 64-67, 75, 122

security considerations, 64
self-interest, 48, 64, 120
self-reliant, 119
Seljuk Turks, 12
Senate, 61-62
sensational, 69
sensitive, 38, 122-123
separates, 5
September 11, 2001, 56, 100
Serbia, 15, 36, 54
sermon, 95, 127
settlements, 36, 42-43
Shah of Iran, 33, 44, 65, 91
Shamir, Yitzhak, 44
shareholders, 38
Sharia, 20, 112-113
Sharon, Ariel, 43
Shatila, 42-43
Shia, 12
shift in power, 4
siege, 3, 26, 134
Sind, 5
sisters, 20, 118
Six-Day War, 33
social equity, 117
social programs, 23
social structure, 16
South Lebanon, 36
sovereignty, 78
Soviet Union, 5, 31, 34-35, 46-47, 135
Spain, 2, 5-6, 13-15, 101, 104, 133-134
split, 14, 127

spread of Islam, 2, 5, 8, 102
spreading religion, 107
stable governments, 13, 65
state-of-the-art weapons, 35
state-sponsored terrorism, 50, 124
stereotyped, 62, 69, 125, 129
stereotyping, 46, 68, 98, 100, 129
Stinger missile, 35
stopped, 5, 36, 47
Strait, 5
strategic options, 79
strategic plans, 47
strategically positioned, 31-32
strategist, 39
students, 22, 79, 95
studies, 22
subjugated, 16
succession rights, 18
Suez Canal crisis, 41, 134
suicide, 37, 56-57, 63, 82, 85, 109-110, 112
suicide pilots, 56
Suleiman, 15
sultan, 27
Sunni, 14, 91
superior, 34, 37, 121, 129
superpower, 35, 71
suppress, 31, 44, 49
suppressed ruthlessly, 35
surviving member, 6
swing vote, 129
symptoms, 115

Syria, 4, 6, 12-13, 16-17, 28-29, 65, 91, 109, 134
Taliban, 55-56, 72, 84, 94-95
talk show, 45-46, 129
Tamerlane, 13, 103
targeted assassinations, 42, 50
technology, 6, 34, 40, 51, 116, 138
Temple Mount, 43
tenets of Islam, 76, 100
terrorism, 46-47, 49-50, 64, 82, 108-113, 124, 128-129
Third World, 65
threat, 13, 16, 32, 39, 75, 112
tolerance, 81, 104, 113, 132
tool of oppression, 106
torture, 31, 42, 50, 91
traditional, 16, 112-113
traditions, 20, 45
TransJordan, 16-17
translate, 7, 54
Transoxania, 5
trends, 19
tribal, 35, 94
trigonometry, 9
Tudeh, 33
Tunisia, 4, 15, 17, 28
Turkey, 6, 12, 15, 19, 27, 77, 134
Turkmenistan, 12, 35
turning point, 15-16
tyranny, 107, 120, 128
ultraconservative, 34, 96
Umar, 3-4, 9, 101

Ummah, 20, 118
Ummayyad, 4-6, 133
UN, 17, 30-31, 42, 48
UN resolution 242, 48
UN resolutions, 30-31, 42, 48
unbiased, 124
underdeveloped, 18, 117
understanding, 28, 59, 78, 100, 125, 130, 132, 138
unemployment, 67, 113
unfriendly countries, 124
unfriendly nation, 31
unholy wars, 107
un-Islamic, 50, 63, 84, 90, 94, 109
United Arab Emirates, 17, 28, 138
United Kingdom, 19
United Nations, 17, 30-31
United States, 19, 22, 31, 34-35, 37, 39, 56, 68, 138
uplift, 27, 53, 118, 120
Uzbekistan, 12, 35
values, 18, 44-45, 65-66, 68, 112-113, 123, 125, 130
vetoed, 31
victimized, 34, 53
Vienna, 3, 15, 26, 134
Vietnam War, 31, 64, 75
violate, 20, 112
violation of American law, 42
violations of human rights, 31
Wahhabi, 27, 95
Wailing Wall, 32

Wall Street Journal, 97
weak, 4, 14, 79, 117, 128
weakened, 6, 12-13, 117
West Bank, 32-33, 43, 135
Western civilization, 26, 45
westernize, 27
westward spread, 5
white papers, 92
women's rights, 18, 117
world, 6-9, 12, 15-16, 18-22, 25, 27-28, 32, 35-37, 39-40, 44-45, 49, 52-53, 55-60, 64-65, 68, 71-76, 78-79, 81, 83, 85, 87, 90, 93-96, 100, 107, 109-112, 115, 121, 123-126, 128, 130
world leadership, 126
World Trade Center, 56-57, 100, 109
World War I, 15-16, 28
World War II, 28
world-renowned, 9
wrong priorities, 18
Yugoslavia, 36
Yusuf, Hamza, 97, 129
Zia-ul-Haq, 39, 44, 48, 65, 84, 92
Zionism, 16
Zogby International, 22, 138

ABOUT THE AUTHOR

Arshad Khan is a successful author, versatile professional, consultant, and adjunct professor. He has written books in diverse fields including stock market investing, software implementation, chemical engineering (desalination), and performance improvement. He has previously been published by leading publishers—John Wiley & Sons and Elsevier Science Publishers (Reed).

Mr. Khan has traveled widely and lived in five countries including 18 years in the United States. He worked for eight years in two Middle Eastern countries, United Arab Emirates and Saudi Arabia, which has given him a broad perspective of the issues discussed in *Understanding Muslim-West Alienation: Building a Better Future*.

Mr. Khan, who earned both his graduate degrees in engineering and business administration in the United States, has taught a variety of business and information technology courses at the University of California (Berkeley and Santa Cruz Extensions), Golden Gate University (San Francisco, California) and National University (San Jose, California).

0-595-23709-6

Printed in the United States
107766LV00009B/60/A